GUITAR *signature licks*

BRAD PAISLEY

by DAVE RUBIN

RECORDING CREDITS:

Doug Boduch – guitar
Tom McGirr – bass
Scott Schroedl – drums
Warren Wiegratz – keyboards
Jerry Loughney – fiddle
Leroy Deuster – pedal steel guitar
Paul Mahn – banjo

Recorded, mixed, and mastered by
Jim Reith (Beathouse Music)
and Jake Johnson (Paradyme Productions)

ISBN 978-1-4234-8408-0

HAL•LEONARD®
CORPORATION
7777 W. BLUEMOUND RD. P.O. BOX 13819 MILWAUKEE, WI 53213

Visit Hal Leonard Online at
www.halleonard.com

CONTENTS

DEDICATION AND ACKNOWLEDGMENTS

I wish to dedicate this book to Leo Fender, the inventor of the Telecaster. Little did he realize in 1950 the vast array of sounds his modest "plank of wood" could produce in the right hands.

Thanks to Gram Parsons and Clarence White, two exceptional and underrated guitarists who helped introduce the artistic worth of country music to the rock audience in the sixties.

GEAR

Brad Paisley is obsessive about his tone and dedicates more time to gear than the vast majority of his southern-fried contemporaries. He has a large collection of guitars featuring many Teles, including his iconic 1968 paisley-patterned model affectionately known as "Old Pink." In addition, he has a number of Crook Custom Tele-style guitars, including one with a Kinman Broadcaster bridge pickup and a 1956 Strat pickup that he used on the 2006 CMA awards show. Like many of his other axes, it also features a McVay G-bender that allows him to create G-string bends that are quite difficult, if not downright impossible, without the setup. One of his vintage Teles has a 1952 body and a 1957 neck with Hamel pickups and a Glaser G-bender. Other guitars are fitted with B- and D-benders. Paisley often favors Lindy Fralin Blue Special pickups in the bridge and Adder pickups in the neck position of his axes, replacing the stock units in virtually all of his instruments.

He currently runs a rig with four Dr. Z Stingray amp heads that he helped design, a Dr. Z KT45 head, vintage Vox AC30 amps that have been his standbys since the beginning, and speaker cabinets housing Webers and Celestions. He also helped design the Dr. Z Prescription Extra Strength model. Besides his effects rack containing a Line 6 Echo Pro Delay, Modulation Pro, and Filter Pro along with a Valve Train Amplification tube reverb unit, he plays through a long list of stompboxes, including: Fulltone Tube Tape Echo, Xotic Effects RC and AC Boosters, Keeley Modded Baked TS-9, Boss DD-2 Digital Delay, Zendrive, Aqua Puss Analog Delay, Furman Power Conditioner, Boss RV-5 Reverb, Ground Control Pro, and an Axess BS-2 Buffer.

BRAD PAISLEY:
ROCKING THE COUNTRY
By Dave Rubin

The white cowboy hat is the first visual hint that this country guitar slinger is cut from different cloth than his more conservative, conformist black-hatted Nashville contemporaries. Then the charming young man with the matinee idol good looks fires off his—what else?—paisley finish Tele, and all hell breaks loose. However, he is not just fast and "clean as country water" like his string-torturing, "pickin' 'n' grinnin'" predecessors Jimmy Bryant, Joe Maphis, and James Burton, as well as country-jazz guitarist Hank Garland. On the contrary, Brad Paisley is also unique in that he possesses a healthy amount of real rock energy and attitude. Additionally, he owes a huge debt of gratitude to the raucous honky-tonk Bakersfield sound of Buck Owens and Merle Haggard from the early sixties. Tellingly, country music legend George Jones has called Paisley the "torchbearer for traditional country music," and one of Brad's biggest influences is another legendary country singer, George Strait. To say that Paisley does it all is like saying that St. Louis Cardinals slugger Albert Pujols can hit.

Brad Douglas Paisley was born on October 28, 1972, to Sandy and Doug in Glen Dale, West Virginia. His maternal grandfather, Warren Jarvis, was a picker and provided his eight-year-old grandson with inspiration and the ubiquitous vintage Sears Silvertone guitar (with amp in case) as his first instrument. Old grandad also passed on his love of Merle Travis, Chet Atkins, and Les Paul, and by the time Paisley was 10, he was performing in church and the local fraternal organizations like the Rotary Club. Hailed as a prodigy, he formed Brad Paisley and the C-Notes with his guitar teacher, Hank Goddard, in a manner that recalled young country phenom Larry Collins in the fifties and his mentor, virtuoso Joe Maphis. When an executive at radio station WWVA in Wheeling, West Virginia heard his first original song, "Born on Christmas Day," the 12-year-old was invited to appear on "Jamboree USA." Also, in 1984, he would become a regular for the next six years on the Saturday night show, originating from the Capital Music Hall, playing with established artists such as Roy Clark, Little Jimmie Dickens, Ricky Skaggs, George Jones, and the Judds.

After graduating high school in 1990, Paisley enrolled in local West Liberty College before transferring to the Belmont University music business program in Nashville, Tennessee, on a full ASCAP scholarship from 1993–95. The move would prove amazingly fortuitous, as he met in "Music City" his future producer, co-songwriter, and second guitarist Frank Rogers, along with another songwriting partner, Kelley Lovelace, and several future band mates. An internship at ASCAP led to Paisley being offered a songwriting deal with EMI Music Publishing upon graduation, where he wrote "Another You" for David Kersh and co-wrote "Watching My Baby Not Come Back" with David Ball in 1999.

After hearing one of his many demos, Arista Records signed Paisley to a contract in 1999. That same year, he made the first of his 40 appearances on the Grand Ole Opry. His debut album, *Who Needs Pictures*, was released in 2000 and promptly went platinum at #13, while the singles "He Didn't Have to Be" and "We Danced" became the first two of his 14 #1 country hits that eventually stretched to 10 in a row; it also hinted at his heart-stopping instrumental prowess to come via "The Nervous Breakdown." Paisley won the Academy of Country Music award for Top New Male Vocalist of the Year and the Horizon Award from the Country Music Association, along with appearing on The Learning Channel special "Route 66: Main Street America" that also featured Buddy Guy. Surprisingly, he performed the classic swing-blues acoustically while being introduced to a national audience for the first time. With the buzz building, he won the Academy of Country Music award for Best New Male Vocalist. As his career picked up speed like a whirlwind, his first Grammy nomination arrived in 2001 for Best New Artist along with induction into the venerable and conservative Grand Ole Opry. In 2002, he followed up his debut album with *Part II*, containing his third #1 single, "I'm Gonna Miss Her (The Fishin' Song)," which won the CMA's Country Music Video of the Year Award. The album leaped to #3 and a more than respectable #31 on the *Billboard* Top 200 charts with a title that punningly refers to movie sequels. Respectfully acknowledging his relationship to the Opry and traditional country music, George Jones, Buck Owens, and Bill Andersen guested on "Too Country."

In 2003, his third album, *Mud on the Tires*, rolled out as his first to reach #1 on the country charts and a robust #8 on the *Billboard* Top 200 on the strength of the title track (#1 and #3), "Little Moments" (#2 and #35), "Celebrity" (#3 and #31), and "Whiskey Lullaby" (#3 and #41) featuring Alison Krauss. In addition, "Whiskey Lullaby" won Vocal Event of the Year and Video of the Year from the Academy of Country Music. A special treat for guitar freaks was Paisley's six-string collaboration with blues and country guitar virtuoso Redd Volkaert on the double-dynamite duet of "Spaghetti Western Swing." Proving his growing "celebrity," the video for "Celebrity" included celebrities William Shatner, Jason Alexander, and Jim Belushi; Paisley later guested on Shatner's record, *Has Been*.

The fourth time was the charm, however, as Paisley busted out with a sensational release and a further display of his full potential. *Time Well Wasted*, in 2005, likewise shot to #1 on the country charts along with #2 on the *Billboard* Top 200 and won the CMA award for Album of the Year and the Academy of Country Music award for Album of the Year. Additionally, the ACM also honored him with Vocal Event of the Year and Video of the Year for "When I Get Where I'm Going." Paisley placed an amazing five songs in the *Billboard* Hot 100 with "Alcohol" (#28), "When I Get Where I'm Going" (#39) with Dolly Parton, "She's Everything" (#35), "The World" (#81), and "Waitin' on a Woman" (#44). Also included was "Out in the Parking Lot" with Alan Jackson. In addition, the sizzling instrumental "Time Warp" showed off his ever-expanding instrumental chops, and he even contributed two songs to the soundtrack of the Disney animated film, *Cars*.

Covering all bases and servicing all sectors of his constituency, in 2006, Paisley released *A Brad Paisley Christmas*, a collection of standards and originals that reached #8 on the country charts and #47 on the *Billboard* Top 200. He came roaring back in 2007 with *5th Gear*, his fifth album of original material and a paean to cars that sported the #1 novelty track "Ticks." The album went on to go #1 on the country charts in addition to #3 *Billboard* Top 200 while winning his first Grammys for "Throttleneck" (Best Country Instrumental) and "Letter to Me" (Best Male Vocal performance). The ACM chipped in with the Top Male Vocalist of the Year Award and Video of the Year for "Online."

Play: The Guitar Album came along in 2008 with a selection of mostly guitar instrumentals and the hit country vocal "Waitin' on a Woman," featuring a cameo by Andy Griffith, added as a bonus track for the faithful. It also hit #1 country and #9 on the *Billboard* Top 200 charts while winning his third Grammy for the awesome "Cluster Pluck" (Best Country Instrumental Performance), which contains a slew of famous guest country guitarists. Clearly produced to feature his exceptional Tele-tickling ability and versatility, the album also contains a blues duet with B.B. King on "Let the Good Times Roll" as well as the stomping hoedown "Kentucky Jelly." On top of that, he pays tribute to Les Paul with "Les is More," Eric Johnson with "Cliffs of Rock City," Joe Satriani with "Kim" and "Departure," and even surf music with the punning "Turf's Up." The autobiographical "Start a Band," a duet with his buddy Keith Urban, hit #1 country and #55 on the *Billboard* Top 100 and copped Vocal Event of the Year from the ACM. Paisley also won CMA awards for Male Vocalist of the Year and for his video of "Waitin' on a Woman" in 2008, along with an American Music Award for Favorite Country Male Artist and the ACM award for Top Male Vocalist of the Year once again. "Waitin' on a Woman" also took home the award for Video of the Year from the ACM.

Racking up the wins year after year, Paisley put out *American Saturday Night* in 2009, which, yet again, went #1 country and #2 on the *Billboard* Top 200 charts and included the #1 country single "Then," his fourteenth chart-topper and tenth consecutive to date. Though more laid-back than previous albums and containing some "blasphemous" synthesizer in a genre loyal to real "analog" stringed instruments, his always aggressive guitarwork keeps the adrenalin flowing even while his country fan base respectfully acknowledges his ongoing musical evolution. In July 2009, Paisley performed in Washington, D.C., in conjunction with "Country Music at the White House." He was also nominated for seven CMA awards in 2009, winning Musical Event of the Year and Male Vocalist of the Year. For the second year, he was co-host along with Carrie Underwood on the November TV broadcast where he took a well-deserved shot at rapper Kanye West for the latter's appallingly disrespectful treatment of 19-year-old country singer Taylor Swift on the 2009 MTV Video Awards program. At a youthful and virile 38 years of age, the phenomenal talent that is Brad Paisley is just entering what promises to be the long and productive primetime of his life.

ALCOHOL

(*Time Well Wasted*, 2005)
Words and Music by Brad Paisley

The history of popular music is besotted with drinking songs—from "John Barleycorn," an ancient English folk ditty famously interpreted by Traffic in 1970, to "What Made Milwaukee Famous (Made a Loser Out of Me)," penned by noted Nashville songwriter Glenn Sutton in 1968 for Jerry Lee Lewis. However, Brad Paisley may be the first to write one from the point of view of the spirits themselves that includes the wry lyric "…and helpin' white people dance."

Figure 1—Verse

The 16-measure verse is comprised of two identical eight-measure sections of B5 (I), E (IV), B5, E, B5–F#/A# (V), G#m (VI)–B5, F#5–F#sus4, and F#. Matching his laconic singing approach, Paisley subtly mixes sustained chords, arpeggios (broken chords), bass lines, chordal fills, and lead licks that flow as natural as beer on tap. Observe how he increases the momentum in measure 6 over the G#m–B5 changes with arpeggios and measure 8 over the F# chord with twangy, vibratoed bass-string licks. In measure 10 over the E chord, Paisley inserts a slippery run in the open position of the E minor pentatonic scale with a crucial substitution of the G# (3rd) that nails down the major tonality. Following the sustained B5 in measure 11, he comes back with slinky, pedal steel-type licks in measure 12 over the E chord that imply E major to Esus4 for tension. By measures 15 and 16 over the F# change, he winds back down with vibrant bass licks from the F# major pentatonic scale.

Performance Tip: Though Paisley employs a G-bender, which makes things considerably easier, it is possible to execute the hip pedal steel licks in measure 12 by placing the ring finger on string 2 at fret 9 and bending string 3 with the index finger. This daunting task is made easier with light gauge strings. Add in the A note at fret 10 on string 2 with the pinky.

Fig. 1

make you   pick a fight   with some-bod - y twice ___   your size. ___

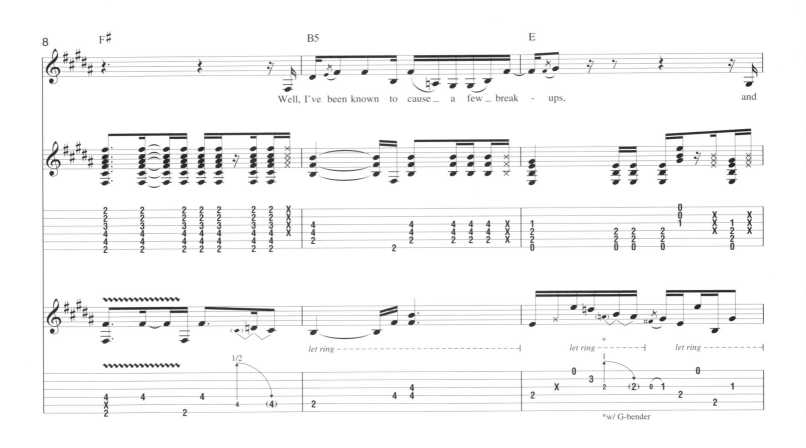

Well, I've been known to cause ___ a few ___ break - ups,   and

*w/ G-bender

ALCOHOL

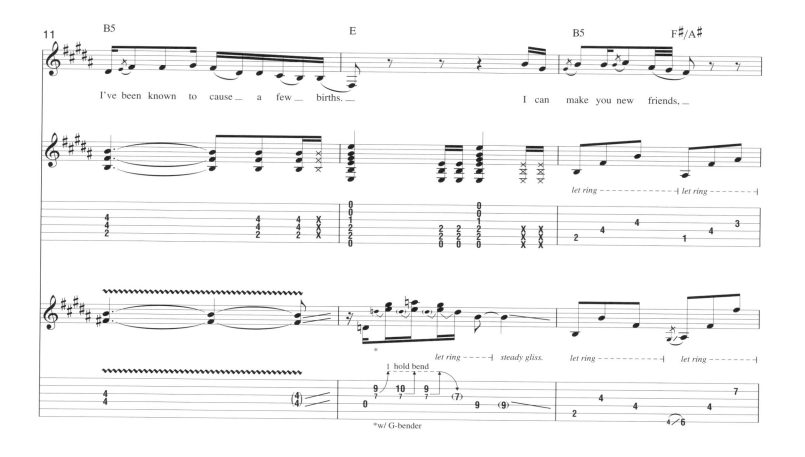

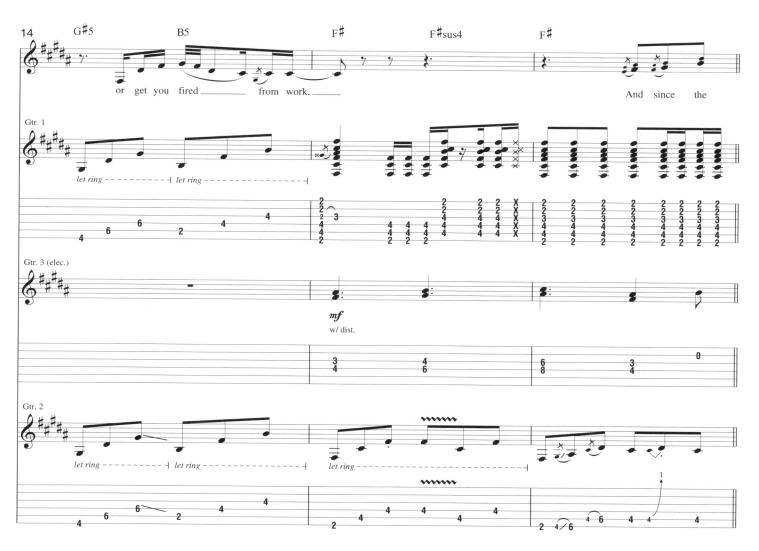

Fig. 2—Outro-Guitar Solo

Paisley possesses enormous chops in conjunction with extensive scale and harmonic knowledge, and he serves up a hefty helping of each in his extended outro solo over a classic I (B5)–IV (E) vamp through the fade in measure 16. Inasmuch as I–IV vamps derive from blues and R&B music, it's therefore appropriate that Paisley engages in a loose form of "call and response" via a chorus responding with "Alcohol" on the E chords along with his wildly improvisational guitar. Be advised that during the course of the solo he gives out with his whole "show," holding nothing back. After establishing the key of B with the most minimal of means via the B (root) note on string 5 at fret 2 in measure 1, he finds a comfortable "home" in the root position of the G♯ minor pentatonic scale that is often seen as the relative minor, or "Nashville scale," by country guitarists and the B major pentatonic scale by rock guitarists. Check out the most useful lick of the scale position in measures 2 and 3 over the E and B5 changes as Paisley bends the C♯ to D♯ on string 3 at fret 6, where it functions as the major 7th of E and the 3rd of B, respectively, for a smooth, consonant sound. In measures 4–7, however, he switches seamlessly to the B blues scale in the root position and unloads several potent musical "rounds" from his Tele. Be sure to see how he does not shy away from the ♭5th (F) on string 3 at fret 10, one of the defining and grittiest notes from the blues scale. In addition, pay attention to and enjoy the sheer exuberance of his awesome salvo in measure 6. Consisting of clusters of blinding thirty-second notes, sextuplets, and quintuplets, it is an early climactic highpoint in the solo and the logical conclusion to the momentum that had been slowly building.

Intelligently, Paisley dynamically turns his direction "on a dime" to dyads in measures 7 and 8 over the B5 and E chords. In fact, besides inserting a taste of harmony while relaxing the taut musical tension of measure 6, the B/A (5th/4th) dyad at fret 12 over the E chord also provides Paisley with an advantageous hand position for his next series of musical ideas. Beginning on beat 2 of measure 8, following mandolin strumming on B/A, he bends the A note a quarter step in conjunction with the fretted B for a brief, but extremely dissonant, tonality that involves the A being bent to B against the D (♭7th) for a helping of classic blues harmony. Not content with results that many other guitarists would readily accept and move on, Paisley creates a cacophony, glissing up the fingerboard with more frenetic mandolin strumming to fret 19 while maintaining the bend to create F♯/D♯ (9th/7th), which he repeats on beat 1 of measure 9 over the B chord to become 5th/3rd for resolution through major tonality. Letting his imagination continue to run rampant with one surprising maneuver after another, he strums F♯/C/A♯ (2nd/♭6th/♯4th) over the E chord in measure 10 for a nasty dissonance that creates harsh, startling musical tension in contrast to what preceded. Adding to the corrosive sound is the gliss of C/D to F♯/E and beyond that finds Paisley repeating F♯/D♯ (5th/3rd) at fret 19 over the B chord in measure 11 for a diatonic resolution. He then continues into measure 12 over the E chord with what could be seen as the B Mixolydian scale fueled by sweet, lyrical blues phrasing, and harmonious note selection.

Warming up to the effect and sailing with a stiff breeze at his back to the end of his solo, Paisley transitions to the root-octave position of the G♯ Aeolian mode, the "true" relative minor scale, in measures 13 and 14 over the I–IV changes. Rather than going out in a slashing blaze of virtuosity, he instead wends his way down the scale with graceful sixteenth-note triplets that tend to slow the perceived passage of time in anticipation of the gradual fade out. It is then tempered by a fast, scratchy rake across strings 4, 3, and 2 for the A, D, and F♯ notes in the root position of the B minor pentatonic scale for a gutsy, blues effect to not appear too "vanilla." Ultimately, Paisley riffs away measure 16, hitting the E (root) note with the D (♭7th), B (5th), and F♯ (9th) notes for resolution and a blues-approved move in idiomatic acknowledgment of the provenance of the chord changes.

Performance Tip: Keep an eye out for the use of open strings within Paisley's single-note runs. A common country guitar maneuver, it provides an "opening" to jump to a new position while adding some pleasing country "twang."

Fig. 2

Outro-Guitar Solo

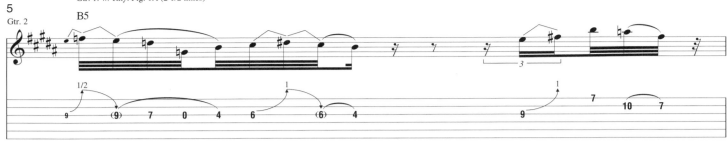

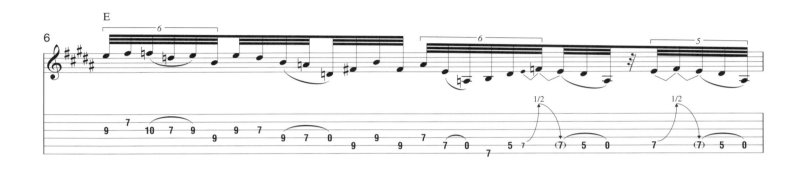

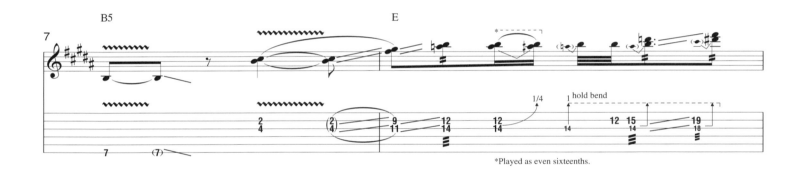

*Played as even sixteenths.

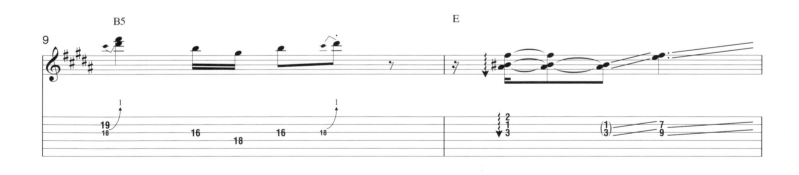

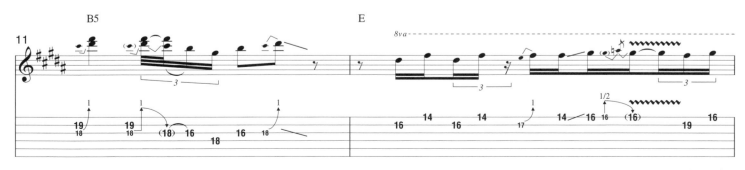

ALCOHOL

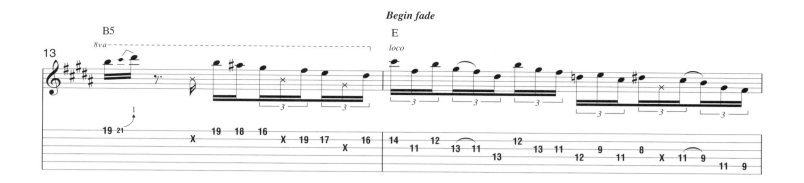

CLUSTER PLUCK
(*Play: The Guitar Album*, 2008)
By Brad Paisley, Frank Rogers and Kevin "Swine" Grantt

Who better to convene a conference of esteemed country guitar hotshots than "young buck" Brad Paisley? Steve Wariner, Albert Lee, Redd Volkaert, John Jorgenson, Vince Gill, Brent Mason, and James Burton all contribute "signature" solos on this landmark instrumental that features Paisley respectfully imitating them, while also playfully throwing down the gauntlet to announce his right to a "seat at the table." Note the sly play on words in the title that, in its original incarnation, refers to an especially ribald situation.

Figure 3—Section A

Paisley (Gtr. 1) invents a popping 16-measure "head" to set the steely "tone" with his Tele and jumpstart the "fast as a tricked-out Dodge Charger" instrumental. Over two eight-measure progressions of A7#9 (I), A7#9, A7#9, A7#9, A7#9, A7#9, F5 (bVI), and G5 (bVII) changes, he plumbs the root position of the A minor pentatonic scale for his melody. The results are a series of seemingly simple, blues-based, one-measure riffs that benefit greatly from the twang of the open strings. Observe how measures 1–6 could be seen as a "call" that creates musical tension over the funky A7#9 (the "Hendrix chord") and that measures 7–8 are the "response" where conclusive resolution occurs on the root note (A) as the open fifth string. Measures 9–14 likewise could be the "call," while measures 15–16, though similar to measures 7–8 and still operating as the "response," actually end on the C (b3rd) note, which Paisley utilizes to smoothly access a gliss up string 5 into section B (not shown).

Performance Tip: Employ just the index and ring fingers for measures 1–6 and 9–14. The muted notes, identified by an "X," may be executed by quickly dropping the palm of the right hand onto the appropriate string and removing it just as quickly in order to pick the notes that follow.

6 Full Band

7 Slow Demo
Gtr. 1   meas. 5–8, 13–16

Fig. 3

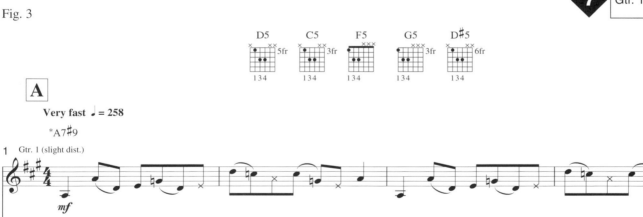

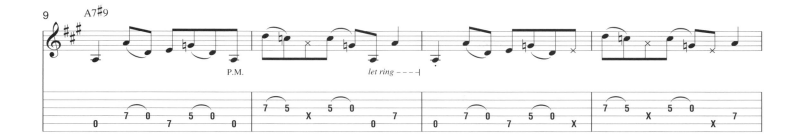

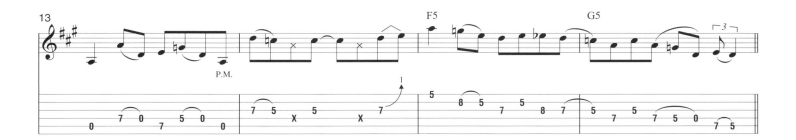

Figure 4—Section D

Steve Wariner was born in Indiana in 1954 and was invited to join the band of Dottie West on bass when he was 17. In 1977, his former bandleader, Chet Atkins, signed him to RCA Records, but when he switched to MCA in 1984, his career really took off with 18 consecutive Top 10 hits. In addition, he has won Grammys for Best Country Vocal Collaboration ("Restless" with Ricky Skaggs in 1991) and for Best Country Instrumental ("Bob's Breakdown" with Asleep at the Wheel in 1999).

After the boss takes his first extended turn, Wariner (Gtr. 2) begins the orgy of Tele pickers over the appointed eight-measure progression of A5 (I), A5, A5, A5–G5 (♭VII), A5, A5, F5 (♭VI)–C5 (♭III), and G5–D5 (IV), with measures 1–6 in dynamic stop time. The changes go by fast at this blistering tempo, and Wariner, like his *compadres*, makes the most of his allotted time. In measures 1 and 2, he descends the harmonious A composite blues scale, neatly dividing the phrase into the minor pentatonic (plus the 9th, B) side in measure 1 and the major pentatonic side in measure 2. In measure 3, he quickly relocates to the root position of the A Mixolydian mode at fret 4 while including the F (♭6th) on string 2 as a chromatic passing tone between E and F♯ that produces another level of fluidity in the solo. It's a short step, both literally and theoretically, to the A composite blues scale at fret 5 in measure 4 that Wariner utilizes for solid resolution to the A note.

Measures 5–8 continue to show his scale mastery and exceptional creativity within severely circumscribed parameters. In measure 5, he skips up through an A major arpeggio of E (5th), A (root), C♯ (3rd), and E, preceding each note by a half step for jagged, dynamic contrast to the smooth phrasing of measures 1–4. Measure 6 contains a loopy run from the A Mixolydian mode that studiously avoids the root and ends on the C♯ to engender a degree of anticipation. As expected, measures 7–8, with the band charging underneath, contain the "best for last" as Wariner ascends through the C♯ (♭5th of F), E (3rd of C), F (♭7th of G), and G (4th of D) notes. The eyebrow-raising sequence produces intense anticipation and musical tension that is logically resolved to the root in measure 1 of the Albert Lee solo (section E).

Performance Tip: Use the index and middle fingers for the ascending pattern in measure 5.

Fig. 4

D

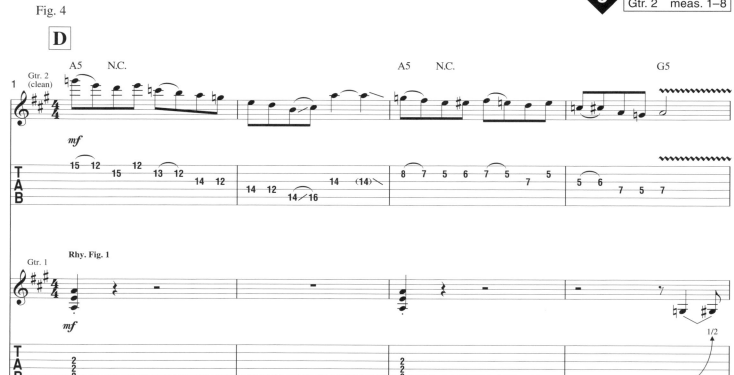

CLUSTER PLUCK

Figure 5—Section E

Albert Lee was born in 1943 in England. Although initially attracted to the fifties rock 'n' roll of Buddy Holly, he soon turned his attention to country music and the hot picking of Jimmy Bryant and James Burton. He first made his name in Heads, Hands & Feet in London before settling in Los Angeles in the early seventies, where he became a sensational session guitarist and eventually inaugurated a solo career. He won a Grammy in 2002 for Best Country Instrumental Performance with "Foggy Mountain Breakdown."

Lee (Gtr. 3) rolls down and then up in register with mostly eighth notes that sparkle like a long string of perfectly-formed pearls. In measures 1–3, he gracefully curls his way down the root position of the A composite blues scale (Mixolydian mode plus blues scale), ending on the open fifth string (A). Beginning on beat 3 of measure 3, however, he rumbles around on the bass strings in the open position of the scale, emphasizing the twang of his Tele along with providing the sonic "low point" of his solo for dramatic dynamics. Check out how the fast bass notes blend together to produce a diatonic harmony in measure 5 with notes from the A major scale that sound more like a piano than guitar.

Even more impressive is the way Lee decides to reverse direction. Glissing from A at fret 5 on string 6 to C# (3rd) at fret 9, he follows with F# (6th) for more diatonic melody and resolves to the A (root) via the note on string 4 at fret 7, the open fifth string, and a punchy hammer-on from the G (♭7th) to A on string 4. The result makes for a welcome break in the endless serpentine flow of notes, thereby setting up his big finish in the climactic measures of 7 and 8. It is instructive to see that each guitarist approaches this crucial section of the progression differently. In measure 7, Lee picks the F (root) note only under the F change followed by a broken C major triad. In measure 8, he executes a similar parallel move with the B (3rd) preceding the G (root) note under the G change, and followed by a D major arpeggio. Notice how anticipating each measure with the C and D triads helps to increase the forward momentum to the end of the solo. As with Fig. 4, Lee resolves to the A (root) note in measure 9.

Performance Tip: Play the broken triads in measures 7 and 8 by barring with the index finger.

Fig. 5

10 — Full Band

11 — Slow Demo
Gtr. 3   meas. 1–8

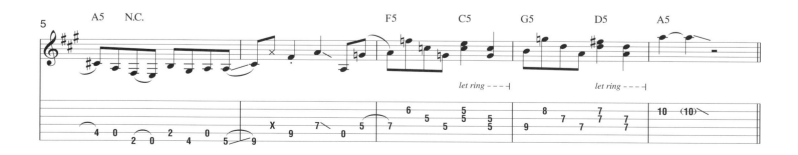

Figure 6—Section F

Redd Volkaert was born in Canada in 1958. His early influences were Merle Haggard, Buck Owens, Led Zeppelin, Deep Purple, Albert King, and Johnny Winter. In 1986, he headed south to Los Angeles with Nashville being his ultimate goal. He further honed his country chops in Music City with the renowned Don Kelley Band and a long list of other artists until Merle Haggard called on him in 1997 to become a Stranger. In 2000, he moved to his current residence in Austin, Texas, for a more "progressive" music scene and gigs locally while playing numerous dates with the old "Okie from Muskogee," among others. He has released three solo albums to date, and Paisley acknowledges him as a major influence.

Volkaert (Gtr. 4) takes an entirely different approach from his fellow Tele-spankers. As opposed to long, mercurial major pentatonic runs, he instead offers syncopated dyads that gain their effectiveness as much from rhythm as from melody and harmony. Measure 1, however, does begin with large intervallic leaps from the A major scale and, for country music, a somewhat unusual 5th dyad of D/G♯ (4th/7th). By the time he gets to measure 2, he is romping mostly with 3rds derived from the A Mixolydian mode through measure 6. As his dyad choices tend to convey musical tension, Volkaert inserts the classic 4th of E/A at fret 5 to establish the A tonality, as in measure 2, and for brief resolution, as in measures 3 and 5. In addition, he also relies on the A (root) on string 4 at fret 7 in measure 4 that also serves to provide phrasing variety. Surprisingly, after the rich trove of harmony in measures 1–6, he utilizes basic major triads relative to the F, C, G, and D changes in measures 7 and 8 to cap his solo. The result is a dynamic change in direction as well as texture. Be aware that he ends on the open fifth (A) string in measure 9.

Performance Tip: Use the middle and index fingers (low to high) for the diagonal dyads, and barre with the index finger for the parallel forms.

Fig. 6

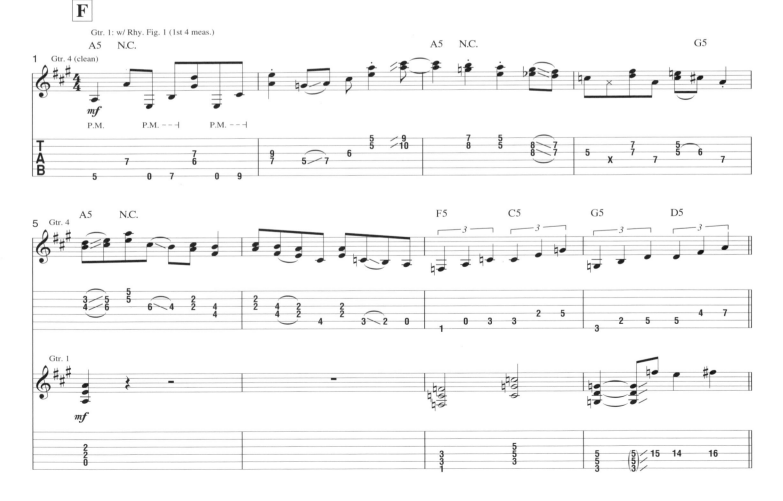

Figure 7—Section G

John Jorgenson was born in Madison, Wisconsin, in 1956, but grew up in Southern California. He studied classical music as a child and became proficient on guitar, mandolin, saxophone, bassoon, and clarinet. The latter was particularly significant as Jorgenson's father was an arranger for Benny Goodman. The youngster once played with the "King of Swing" and enjoyed a gig at Disneyland. In 1986, he convened the Desert Rose Band, which was named Touring Band of the Year 1988–90 by the Academy of Country Music. On a lark, in 1992, he formed the wild and wooly Hellecasters with fellow virtuosos Jerry Donahue and Will Ray, producing three instrumental albums and becoming instant cult guitar heroes.

Jorgenson (Gtr. 5) literally takes the "high road" by initiating his jaunt with the A Mixolydian mode at fret 17. In measures 1 and 2, he palm mutes an A major arpeggio from the scale that draws in the listener with some repetitive staccato upper-register picking. Accelerating quickly in measure 3, he glides fluidly down the fingerboard through measure 8 with numerous glisses, hammers, and pulls that are the sonic equivalent of shooting the rapids in a raft. Observe how he shifts positions in every measure, creating steady anticipation that adds to the forward momentum along with the descending runs. At the same time, except for measure 3, he manages to include the A (root) note in every measure in order to maintain a sense of tonality in the midst of the onrushing improvisation. Check out how Jorgenson displays great skill in measures 7 and 8 by subtly including the root note of each change at the appropriate juncture without interrupting the relentless forward motion of his solo.

14 Full Band

15 Slow Demo
Gtr. 5   meas. 1–8

Fig. 7

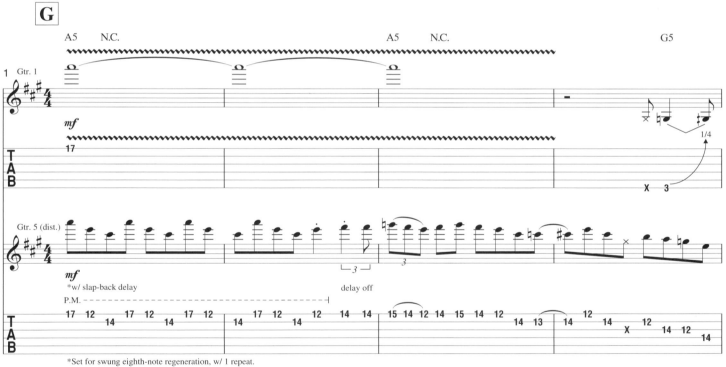

*Set for swung eighth-note regeneration, w/ 1 repeat.

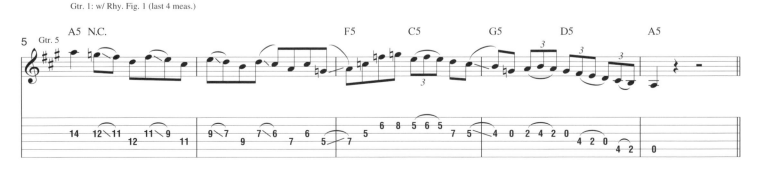

Figure 8—Section H

Vince Gill was born in Oklahoma in 1957. His musician father encouraged his talent, and Gill studied violin and piano, eventually learning guitar, mandolin, fiddle, Dobro, and bass. His band years started in 1975 when he moved to Louisville, Kentucky, to play bass and guitar with Ricky Skaggs and Jerry Douglas in Boone Creek before heading to Los Angeles, where he joined Byron Berline in Sundance. In 1979, he passed an audition for Pure Prairie League, staying with them for three albums. He signed a contract with RCA in 1983 and moved to Nashville where he became a session guitarist. Gill switched labels to MCA in 1989 and won the first of his 14 Grammys, tying him with Chet Atkins for most by a country artist, to go along with his record 18 Country Music Association awards.

Gill (Gtr. 6) is probably the bluesiest "Nashville cat" out of the group of illustrious guest stars showing their wares on "Cluster Pluck." Hence, he leans heavily on the A major pentatonic scale, voiced as F♯ minor pentatonic at fret 2 where the "blues licks" lie, and the root position of the A minor pentatonic scale at fret 5. Similar to Redd Volkaert, Gill utilizes striking, rhythmic syncopation in his solo as much as note selection and melody, eschewing long, winding runs in the process. In measures 1–6, he hammers, pulls, and bends notes from the A major pentatonic scale, often skipping strings and incorporating open strings for a jumping, dynamic effect. Check out the classic major pentatonic move of B (2nd) bent one step to C♯ (major 3rd) in measures 2 and 3 that is a favorite of country pickers. The exceedingly cool, repeating pull-offs of C♯/A to the open third string (G) and the G note on string 4 at fret 5 in measures 5 and 6, however, are a Gill trademark and are well worth copping for future applications!

Flashing his blues credibility, Gill bends the C (♭3rd) a quarter step to the "true blue note" in measure 6 before launching into a classic blues run with roots back to T-Bone Walker and B.B. King in measures 7 and 8. Also including the E♭ (♭5th) from the A blues scale across the bar line, the phrase emphasizes the A in measure 8 before resolving over the A change in measure 1 of section I. Be sure to see that Gill blows right over the last four changes in measures 7–8 for musical tension, like a true bluesman on the way to the finish line for resolution, as opposed to his predecessors who tend to delineate the harmony.

Performance Tip: For the pull-offs in measures 5 and 6, barre strings 3 and 2 at fret 2 with the index finger and use the pinky for the G note at fret 5 on string 4.

Fig. 8

Figure 9—Section J

Brent Mason was born in Ohio in 1959. Considered a child prodigy, at five he was sliding a kitchen knife across the strings of his father's acoustic guitar and would go on to have wide, eclectic tastes from Hank Williams to James Taylor and Jeff Beck. His first trip to Nashville in the early seventies resulted in failure. However, on a second trip in 1981, he scored a steady gig with the house band at the famous Stagecoach Lounge. Chet Atkins saw him there and was so knocked out that he returned with George Benson and invited Mason to be one of several guest artists on his album *Stay Tuned* in 1985. The buzz built, and he became the hottest Nashville session guitarist as well as firing up the band of mega-star Alan Jackson. The Academy of Country Music named him Guitarist of the Year from 1993–98. It is possible that Mason is the most recorded guitarist in history.

Mason combines the D composite blues scale (Mixolydian mode plus blues scale) and assorted chromatic runs in a stunning display of super-smooth virtuosity. Rather than beginning above the octave and descending like some of his peers, he instead starts around fret 8 and breathlessly phrases in discrete but related chunks as he twists and turns down the fingerboard until he ends up in the open position in measure 6. Similar to John Jorgenson (Fig. 7), he includes the D (root) note in each measure of 1–6 to maintain tonal focus. High points include the pedal steel-type licks in measure 1, the slinky half-step bend from F (♭3rd) to F♯ (major 3rd) across the bar line in measures 2–3, and the exceptionally-hip, descending and ascending chromatic lines back-to-back in measures 3–4. Observe that Mason walks a fine line (pun intended!) between literally outlining each change and just bulling his way through them in measures 7 and 8. Starting at the third position of the composite blues scale on string 6 with the G note, he traverses vertically across the strings, nipping the C and G root notes in the bud. He also includes a chromatic passage of B♭–B–C–C♯ on string 3, beats 1 and 2 of measure 8 that then connects to string 3 for D–D♯–E to coincide with the chord changes, including the E7 that follows.

Fig. 9

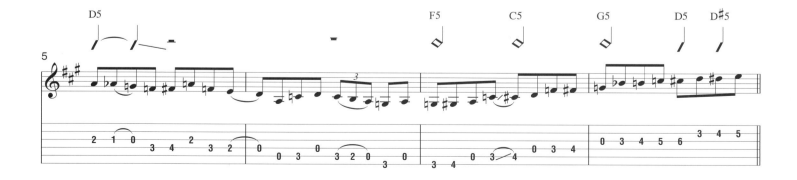

Figure 10—Section K

The "elder statesman" of modern country-rock guitarists, James Burton was born in Louisiana in 1939. By the age of 14, he was playing clubs and parties and was asked to join the famous "Louisiana Hayride." In 1955, the 15-year-old was with Dale Hawkins and played the signature intro to "Susie-Q." Relocation to Hollywood for a movie part led to him appearing in the late fifties and early sixties on the "Ozzie and Harriet" TV show in the backing band of young Ricky Nelson. A stint in the house band on the "Shindig!" TV show was followed by session work, including significant collaborations with Buck Owens and Merle Haggard that would contribute to the development of the "Bakersfield sound." In 1969, he was picked by Elvis Presley to join his band in a musical relationship that lasted until the singer's death in 1977, at which time Fender honored him with a paisley-finished Tele. In 2001, he was inducted into the Rock and Roll Hall of Fame by Keith Richards.

Burton (Gtr. 8) is given the rightful respect of a double-length improvisation over a 16-measure progression of E7 (V) for four measures, A7#9 (I) for four measures, E7 for four measures, C6/9 (♭VI) for two measures, and finally two measures of C5–C#5–D5–D#5 and E5–F5–F#5–G5 changes. As opposed to his "protégés," he plays more chordally rather than "scalarly," a characteristic of his style that no doubt dates back to his days in Louisiana when he learned to trade licks with pedal steeler Sonny Trammel. In measures 1–4, he harmonizes around the E7 tonality through a variety of forms to create vertical rather than horizontal movement. Utilizing open strings 2 (B) and 1 (E) as ringing "pedal tones," Burton begins by including the fretted D (♭7th) on string 3 at fret 7. In measures 3 and 4, he expands the harmony by adding the G# (3rd) to the mix to complete the E7 voicing as a broken chord.

In measures 5–8 over the A7 chord, he mixes single notes with dyads and triads, again nailing the tonality in each measure and producing forward motion in contrast to measures 1–4. Starting at the 12th fret, he executes the *de rigueur* country guitar lick of the B (2nd or 9th) bent one step to the C# (3rd) in conjunction with the E (5th). The following C#/A dyad leads handsomely to the triads and dyads in measure 6 that could be seen as G, A, and D voicings from the A Mixolydian harmonized scale. Their function is to lead the ear to resolution on the A chord in measures 7 and 8 with the R&B classic hammer-on of C to C# and the A (root) note from the root position of the A minor pentatonic scale.

Measures 9–12 revert back to E7 and Burton likewise returns to his theme from measures 1–4. Showing his uninhibited creativity, he plays the G# (3rd), B (5th), and D (♭7th) notes on string 3 in conjunction with open strings 2 (B) and 1 (E) to produce a shimmering wash of E and E7 chord tones that, like measures 1–4, emphasize vertical rather than horizontal motion. Wrapping it up in measures 13–16, Burton glisses hip triple-stop voicings in measures 13 and 14, again sounding remarkably like a steel guitarist, and complementing the C6/9 harmony. And not to be outdone by the "whippersnappers" in the last two measures, he picks the individual notes from dyads in 4ths and 3rds (derived from the root position of the A minor pentatonic scale) while scampering from strings 2 and 1 to strings 5 and 4. Observe the vibrant, exciting sound that results from the alternating occurrences of harmony and dissonance with the underlying chord changes.

Performance Tip: Burton (and likewise, Paisley) is a master at "hybrid picking," the fine art of holding a flat pick between the thumb and index finger in the conventional manner while also using the middle and ring fingers to access additional strings for a fingerstyle effect.

Fig. 10

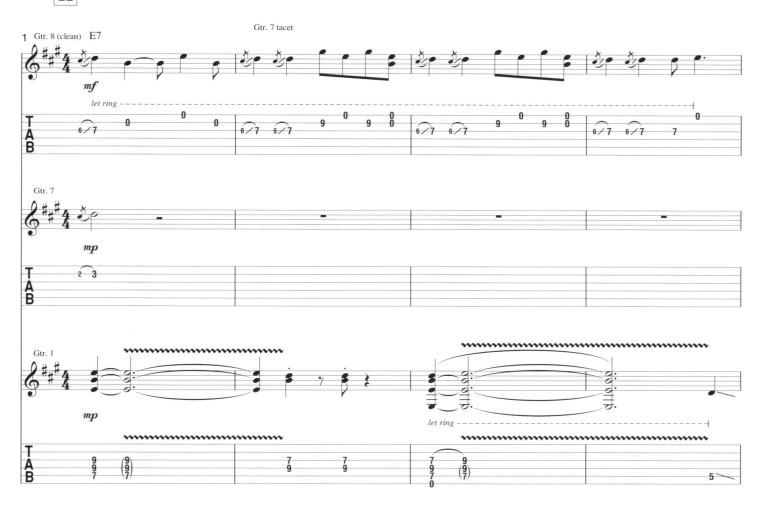

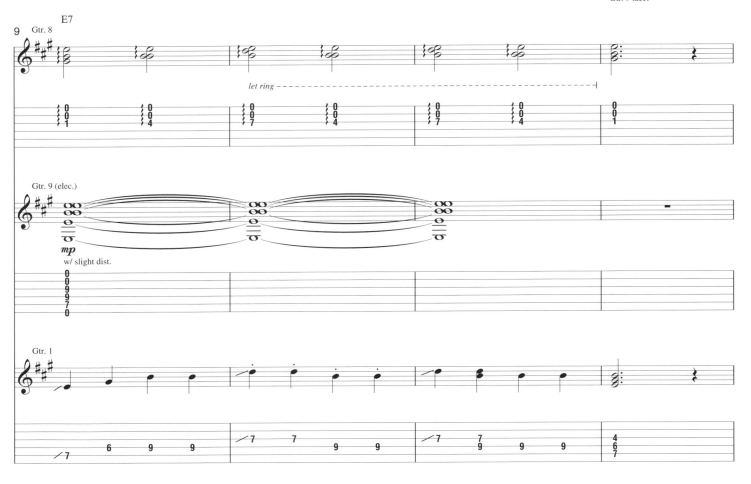

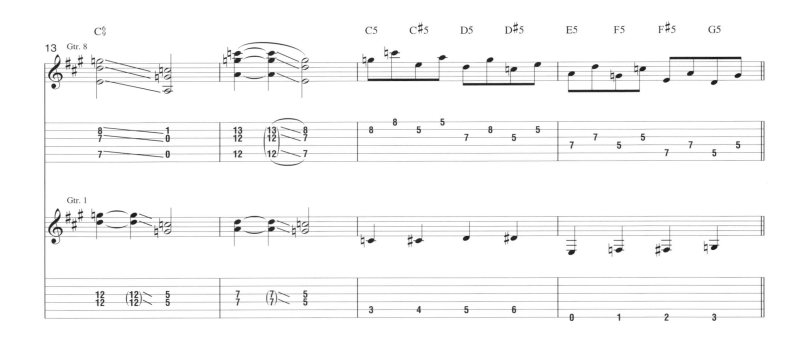

HUCKLEBERRY JAM

(Play: The Guitar Album, 2008)
By Brad Paisley and Frank Rogers

This playful instrumental is named for Paisley's first-born son, William "Huckleberry." It is the first track on the album, and its virtuosity serves notice to guitarists of all stripes that the artist is a man who is not going to keep his "light hid under a bushel basket."

Figure 11—Section B

The 16-measure progression that functions as the "head" of the tune is composed of four four-measure increments. Measures 1–4 and 9–12 consist of A (I), A, A, and E7 (V) chords, while measures 5–8 and 13–16 consist of A, C (♭III)–D (IV), E7, and A changes. Paisley (Gtr. 1), in his inimitable style, lays a rollicking and rolling melody over the A changes that begin each four-measure section with an abundance of triplets and open strings derived from the composite blues scale (Mixolydian mode plus blues scale). Particularly effective are the numerous triplet pull-offs to the open fifth (A), fourth (D), and third (G) strings that zip like laser lights. Observe the chunky E7 chords in measure 4 that add dynamic contrast to the high-powered licks and momentarily stabilize the flood of notes pouring from Paisley's overheated Tele.

In measures 6–8, he navigates the changes through his usual wide variety of means. Starting in measure 6, he utilizes arpeggiated *first inversion* (3rd on the bottom) C and D chords in order to add another welcome dose of harmony. In measure 7 over the E7 chord, he resorts to a melodic line of notes on string 1 derived, appropriately, from the E Mixolydian mode. Ending the section, he combines notes from the A composite blues scale with briefly implied D and C triads for a fat sound that conclusively defines the tonality.

Performance Tip: Brad, like many fast country pickers, uses the hybrid picking (pick and fingers) technique extensively. This allows him much greater speed than just using a pick alone and also assists in the ubiquitous "chicken pickin'" sound that is so prevalent in country guitar.

22 Full Band

23 Slow Demo
Gtr. 1   meas. 1–8

Fig. 11

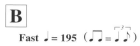

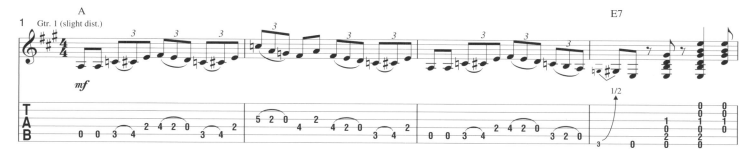

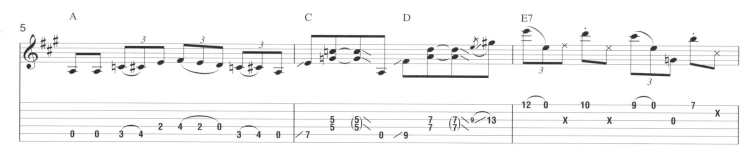

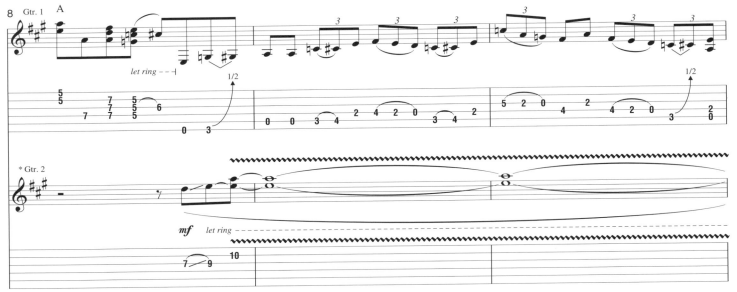

*Pedal steel arr. for gtr.

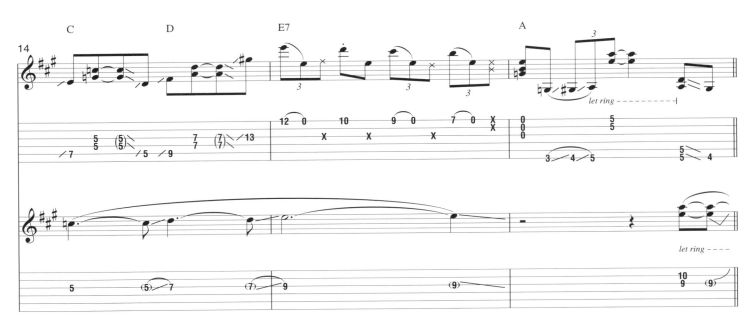

Figure 12—Section E

The first of his improvised solos is played over the same 16-measure progression as found in section B. Hence, Paisley (Gtr. 1) approaches his task in four-measure increments and has a ball ripping around the changes. In measures 1–3, he starts low in the A composite blues scale over the A (I) chords, literally on the open fifth (A) string, and commences to "pickin' the chicken" while making sure to emphasize the A (root), C# (3rd), and E (5th) notes. He acknowledges the E7 (V) in measure 4 by dipping into the E composite blues scale and staying mainly on string 6 for a whomping sound and dynamic change in register. Observe the clever bend from D (♭7th) to D# (major 7th) on beat 4 for an unusual taste of dissonance that ends the section with a sharp jolt.

Measure 5 veers off the track immediately with a run that includes B♭ (♭9th) and D# (#4th) for serious musical tension. He transitions into the root position of the A blues scale in measure 6 where the B♭ (♭7th) and C (root) notes help define the C chord change, and the A/E dyad alludes to a D9 tonality for at least a degree of appropriate harmony. In measures 7 and 8, Paisley radically changes direction once again with an eclectic series of 6th dyads that roughly harmonize with both the A and E changes. More importantly, the chromatic line on string 5 that walks from F# to C, and the breathless speed with which it all is executed, leads "hell bent for leather" to resolution on the A (root) note in measure 9.

Paisley settles into the A composite blues scale at fret 14 in measures 9–11 over the A change for a smoking ride that, harmonically, if not rhythmically, provides a respite from the tension-inducing moves that preceded. Check out the dynamic, careening relocation to the low E string in measure 12 over the E7 chord for a thumping bass-string run that resolves conclusively to an E+ voicing. Heading towards a satisfying climax in measures 13–16, Paisley "chicken picks" his way through the open position of the A minor pentatonic scale for yet another flavor via the gritty, bluesy nature of the scale choice. Pay attention to how he emphasizes the C (root) note on beat 1 of the C–D chords in measure 14 and anticipates the E7 chord coming up in measure 15 with the first (E) and second (B) open strings on beat 4. Pulling a doozy out of his bag of tricks, Paisley closes the show in measure 16 over the A chord by playing an open-position A major triad and *bending* the neck of his Tele for a slick whammy bar "dive bomb" imitation. Whew!

Performance Tip: Play the E9 voicing in measure 12, low to high, with the middle and index fingers and the ring finger as a barre on strings 3 and 2.

Fig. 12

Guitar Solo

*w/ G-bender

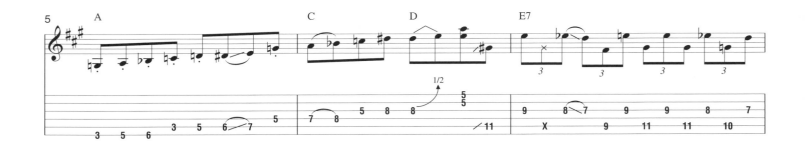

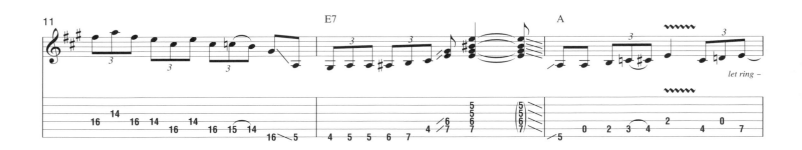

*Bend neck.

I'M GONNA MISS HER (THE FISHIN' SONG)

(Part II, 2002)

Words and Music by Brad Paisley and Frank Rogers

Showing his traditional side, Paisley gets all "Nashville" with this weepy tale of domestic strife. However, lest anyone take it too seriously, he applies his usual lyrical wit to the situation. As the old saying goes, "A bad day fishing is better than a good day working"—or keeping a girlfriend. It hooked #29 on the *Billboard* Hot 100.

Figure 13—Verse

The odd, 11-measure verse is as loopy as the lyric while sounding perfectly normal until it is inspected more closely. With Gtr. 1 picking acoustic broken chords, it is composed of three increments: The first contains four measures of G (I)–G/B, C (IV), D7 (V), and G–D in a standard I, IV, V country progression. The second in measures 5–8 builds anticipation with G–G/B, C–A/C# (II), G–D/F#–Em (vi), and G–D/F#–Em via the "relative minor" chord of G (Em). Measures 9–11 of Asus4–A, D, and D leave the listener hanging on to see what happens in the chorus (not shown) with the extra measure of the V chord intensifying the effect.

Notice how Gtr. 2 embellishes the melody with acoustic slide in open G tuning and how he follows the changes with chord forms in measures 2–6 and 10 by moving his slider to the appropriate fret position. In measures 7–8, however, he complements the harmony with two different single-note lines of B (3rd)–A (5th)–G (♭3rd) and G (root)–F# (3rd)–E (root) over the G–D/F#–Em chords. Likewise, in measure 9, he plays D (4th) over Asus4 and C# (3rd) over the A chord as the defining notes of the harmony.

Performance Tip: It is always good practice to wear the slider on the pinky in order to leave the other fingers free to fret.

Fig. 13

*Symbols in double parentheses are respective to capoed guitars, single parentheses to alternate-tuned guitars.
Symbols above represent actual sounding chords. Chord symbols reflect overall harmony. Capoed fret is "0" in tab.

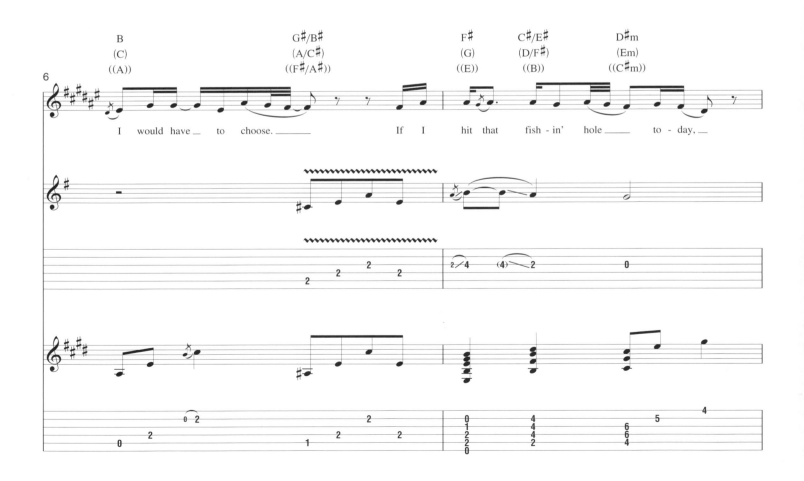

I'M GONNA MISS HER (THE FISHIN' SONG)

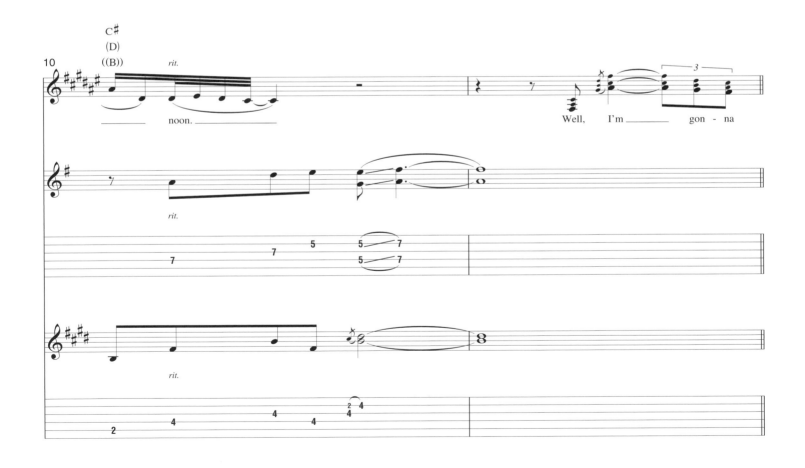

Figure 14—Guitar Solo

Paisley (Gtr. 3) scampers around the chords in the eight-measure solo with his usual exuberance. It contains the same C (IV), C, G (I), G, D (V), D, G, and G changes as measures 1–8 of the chorus, benefitting from the built-in forward motion provided by beginning on the IV chord with eventual resolution to the I chord. Breaking fast out of the gate, he brackets measures 1 and 2 of the C chord with C dyads and triads at fret 5 to establish the tonality. In between the harmonic "bookends," Paisley starts low on the fingerboard and "twangs" throaty bass-string licks, combining notes from the C major scale along with chromatic runs. Before moving on to the G chord in measure 3, he works a cool move from the C major scale at fret 8 by bending the A (6th) to the B (major 7th) and resolving back to the consonant G (5th) that serves double duty by also anticipating the next change.

Paisley shifts to the G Mixolydian mode in measure 3 of the G change, but then, as is his modus operandi, throws a "curve" by evolving into the G composite blues scale in measure 4, while employing the G-bender for ear-twisting variants. It adds a subtle, blues edge to his dynamic return to the squawking bass licks that are a unique characteristic of country Tele-pickers. In measure 5 of the D chord, he, likewise, makes a dynamic change of pace when he just sustains the D (root) and rests as the pedal steel guitarist Randall Currie enters for a spell. After that, through measures 6–8, Paisley plays complementary lines under Currie, including classic blues harmony bends in measure 7 of the G chord of C (4th) to D (5th) against the fretted F (♭7th) for a little spunk. Observe the beautiful unison lines with the pedal steel that Paisley plucks from the G major scale in measure 8 to close out the solo with sweet consonance.

Performance Tip: Paisley is likely employing his G-bender in measure 8 to bend the A to B on beat 1. In lieu of owning a guitar with one installed, it is recommended to pull down vigorously on the A with the index finger.

Fig. 14

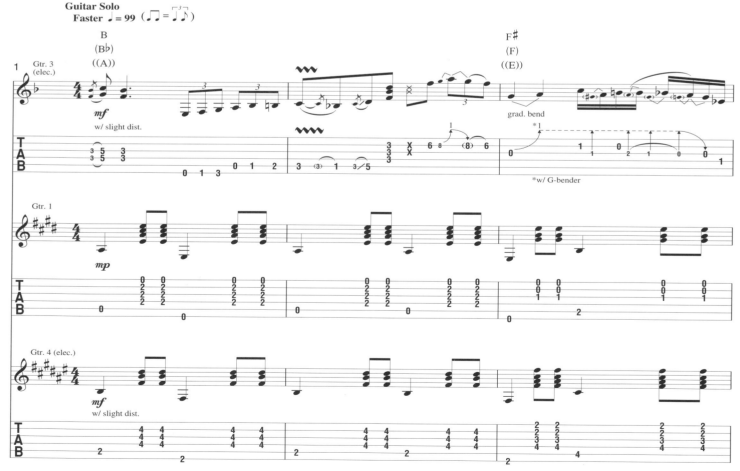

I'M GONNA MISS HER (THE FISHIN' SONG)

MR. POLICEMAN

(*5th Gear*, 2007)
Words and Music by Brad Paisley, Chris DuBois,
Jim Beavers and Jimmie Rodgers

As if Paisley needed one, "Mr. Policeman" offers him a good excuse to really "air it out," and he burns rubber on this high speed "Smokey and the Bandit" tribute. Note that he quotes Jimmie Rodgers' "In the Jailhouse Now," from 1928, in the outro, further lending credibility to his knowledge and genuine respect for the roots of country music. In fact, the song was first copyrighted in 1915 by Davis and Stafford, two African-American performers.

Figure 15—Intro

Paisley (Gtr. 1) flatpicks like an electric bluegrass demon in the 16-measure intro. Basically a I (G)-chord vamp with F5 (♭VII)–G5 and B♭5 (♭III)–F5 changes in measures 7–8 and a dynamic drop down to F5 in measures 15–16, it provides a veritable racetrack for him to test drive his Tele. As Gtr. 1 in measures 1–6 and 8–14 over the G5 chord, he rips numerous zinging pull-offs combined with open strings in what is essentially the G minor pentatonic scale. Notice, however, the open fifth (A) string from the G major scale in measures 4 and 12 that contributes a taste of diatonic nuance to the stripped-down runs.

As he does as a matter of course, Paisley inserts chords where they not only add harmony but dynamic contrast to the carloads of single notes. Logically, this occurs in measures 7 and 8, where he shifts to F5, G5, and B♭5 "power chords" with the added octave on top. Following four more measures of high-octane pull-offs over the G changes, he pumps F (root) notes on string 6 at fret 1 in measures 15–16 over the F5 chord to complete the trip.

Performance Tip: Use the ring finger for the pull-offs on strings 3 and 4 and the index finger for the two pull-offs from B♭ to the fifth string.

29 Full Band

30 Slow Demo
Gtr. 1   meas. 1–4

Fig. 15

Gtr. 3: Drop D tuning:
(low to high) D–A–D–G–B–E

*Chord symbols reflect basic harmony.

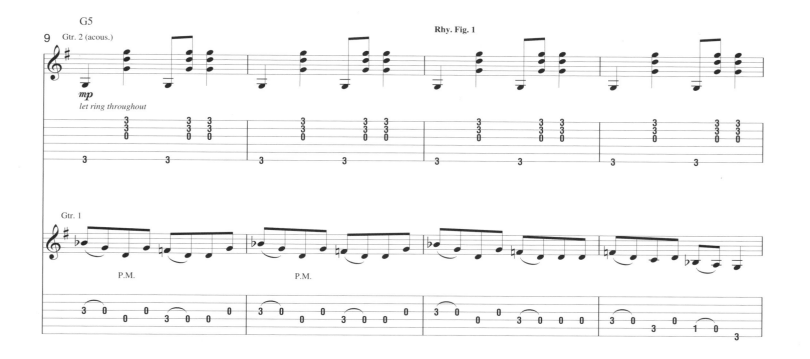

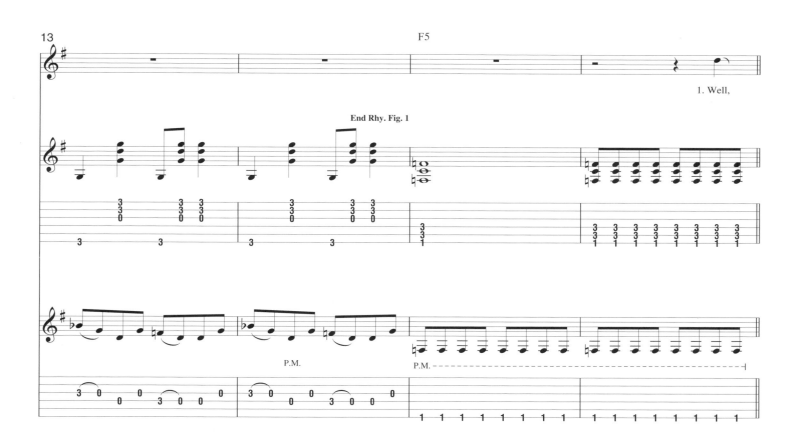

Figure 16—Guitar Solo 1

Paisley fully turns loose his desire to flaunt his justly lauded guitar skills in three skidding, "squealing tire" solos in keeping with the breakneck tempo and lyric conceit of the tune. In the first, he (Gtr. 1) guns his way through alternating four-measure sequences of C (IV), G5 (I), C, and G5 for 16 measures of piston-pounding eighth notes. In measures 1–4, he relies on one of his fave scale choice, the root and open positions of the composite blues scale (Mixolydian mode plus blues scale) in G. In keeping with the chord change, he zeroes in on the C (root) on string 3 at fret 5 along with E (major 3rd) to peg the tonality. Picking on the G (5th) that falls naturally in these scales completes the C major triadic tones.

In measures 5–8 over the G5 chord, Paisley remains in the same scale positions but with a subtle shift of emphasis to the open third (G) and fourth (D) strings for the root and 5th, respectively, and one quick, well-placed B (3rd) on beat 3 in measure 6 that precedes the open third string. Check out the slide from F# (major 7th) to Bb (b3rd) in conjunction with the open 3rd (G) string in measure 7 for a little harmony and texture in contrast to the miles of single notes speeding by like a picket fence. In addition, notice the unadulterated notes from G Mixolydian mode in measure 8 that imply G dominant tonality while the C and G notes on beats 3 and 4 anticipate the change back to C around the curve in measure 9.

Measures 9–10 find Paisley racing up and down through the root position of the C composite blues scale for a welcome change from the previous G scales. In measure 11, he decides to fatten up the sound with 3rd dyads, relative to C major, as a prelude to the brief hit on the C triad in measure 12 to complete the section. However, lest he resolve too comfortably and slow the action, observe the surprising D/Bb (9th/b7th) dyad on beat 3 of measure 12 where he bends (with his G-bender, likely) the Bb a half step to B (major 7th) followed by the G (5th) and F (4th) notes that create a pinch of tension to move the action forward.

In measures 13–16 over the G change, Paisley charges headlong through the G composite blues scale with skittering pull-offs and open strings, providing a fitting end to the thrill ride. Be sure to see the hammer-on from Bb (b3rd) to B (3rd) in measures 15 and 16 that produces a subtle bluesy effect true blues cats would more often play on string 3 at fret 3, but perfectly keeps with classic country picking in the requisite bass frequencies.

Performance Tip: For the "G-bender" bend in measure 12, place the index finger on the D note on string 2 and bend the Bb note on string 3 with the middle finger.

31 **Full Band**

32 **Slow Demo**
Gtr. 1 meas. 1–16

Fig. 16

Guitar Solo

Figure 17—Guitar Solo 2

Paisley (Gtr. 1) kicks his six-string machine into a higher gear in his second guitar solo—if that can be imagined. Where the first solo had a few quarter notes and even a triplet for dynamic contrast, here he blows the doors off the "Smokey" with virtually non-stop eighth notes. The 16-measure progression consists of eight measures of G5 (I), Dsus4 (V), Dsus4, C (IV), G5, Dsus4, Dsus4, C, and a measure of G5–E5 (VI)–F5 (♭VII)–F#5 (#IV).

As expected, Paisley makes his usual spectacular entrance. In measures 1 and 2, he comes in rumbling like a NASCAR racer on the G (root) and F (♭7th) notes on string 6, similar to measures 15 and 16 of the intro. He next accelerates up through the G composite blues scale, incorporating a number of embellishments that contribute to the flat-out forward motion of the solo. Foremost are the chromatic runs in measure 4 that begin with palm muting evolving smoothly to a dynamic volume change. Be sure to see that the run resolves logically to the open third (G) string on beat 1 of measure 5 that also contains a tart dissonance by way of D/Bb (5th/b3rd) pulled of to the open third string and followed by the bluesy Bb. The action sets up the first climax that occurs in measure 6 where Paisley continues ascending to a peak with the G note on string 1 at fret 3. Observe the half-step moves along the way of C (4th) to C# (#4th) and E (6th) to F (b7th) that tend to draw extra attention to the measure through unexpected melodic dissonance.

In measures 9 and 10 over the Dsus4 chord, Paisley shifts from the D major pentatonic scale for consonant harmony to the G composite blues scale, where he emphasizes the Bb (b6th) notes and ends on the G (4th) for musical tension. He maintains the tension in measure 11 over the C change with a brief stop in the C blues scale with the D# (b3rd) and F (4th) prominently working their grit into the proceedings. Then he seamlessly transitions into an exceptionally cool descending chromatic pattern on string 5 (Db–C–B) that includes the alternating notes of E and D on string 4 to imply harmony in bluesy b3rds. Of course, the "method" to Paisley's "madness" is that the chromatic run continues to measure 12 over the G chord, where he plays the Bb and A in sequence on string 5 and reverses direction from the F# to G on string 6 followed by the open third (G) string to unambiguously resolve the breathless musical anticipation.

With one long descending line of eighth notes, Paisley gives it the gas in measures 13–16 in a similar manner to measures 9–12. If anything, he increases the unmistakable sense of forward momentum by restricting his register to fret 5 and below. The result is a more compact, focused sound that still manages to clip the D and C root notes in measures 13–15 from the G composite blues scale. Even more remarkable is the way he includes the F# (major 7th) over G5 and the E (root) over the E5 in measure 16 while utilizing the B (b5th) and D (#5th) over the F5 and F#5 changes, respectively, for tension that does not resolve until measure 1 of the banjo solo (not shown) that follows.

Performance Tip: Try to alternate pick as much as possible for efficiency and speed.

33	Full Band
34	Slow Demo Gtr. 1 meas. 1–16

Fig. 17

Guitar Solo

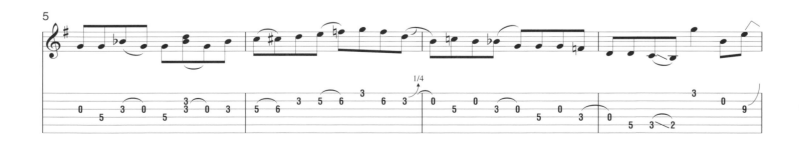

Figure 18—Guitar Solo 3

Flashing his astounding speed, accuracy, and masterful scale command, Paisley (Gtr. 3) kicks his chops into overdrive for his third solo that dramatically and directly precedes the slower tempo of the "In the Jailhouse Now" outro. Contributing to the rubber burning power is the key change up a 5th (D) for eight measures of D (I), followed by A (V), A, G7 (IV), D, A, A, G7, and A for a total of 16.

Measures 1–8 contain an unbroken and fluid "string" of eighth notes mostly derived from the D composite blues scale. However, check out the chromatic run in measures 1–3 on string 6 from A (5th) at fret 5 to E (9th) at fret 12 that Paisley alternates with minor 3rds from C (♭7th) at fret 3 to A (5th) at fret 12 on string 5. When he gets to measure 4, he starts working his way up the fingerboard both vertically and horizontally until he arrives at the seventeenth position in measure 8 where he neatly dovetails with the A (V) changes in measure 9. Dig the unusual lick in measure 9 over the E (5th) on string 2 blended with the B (9th) bent to C♯ (3rd) on string 1 to create a soulful 6th of C♯/E followed by the 4ths of A/E and G/D, providing fat R&B-type harmony, that lead to the A major scale at fret 12 in measure 10.

Showing off his thorough knowledge of his favorite scales in measure 11 over the G7 (IV) chord, Paisley alters the A major scale to become a G major scale with the addition of the C (4th) note at fret 13 on string 2. Observe that the C♯ (♯4th) from the A scale that precedes it is held over in order to allow for a short, descending chromatic phrase of C♯–C–B. Likewise, check out that relocating to around fret 10 puts him in an advantageous position to access the D composite blues scale in the root position, along with the D major pentatonic scale at fret 7, in measure 12 over the D change. Inasmuch as Paisley tries to avoid becoming predictable or programmatic with his scale choices, in measure 13 over the A (V) chord he remains in the D major pentatonic scale. However, his note selection reflects the A (root) and E (5th) tones from the key of A along with the F♯ (6th) and B (9th) tones also relative to D. In measure 14 over the A chord, he anticipates the finish line in measure 16 and, with one last burst of speed, charges down through an altered A major scale. Be aware of the inclusion of the funky B♭ (♭9th) and the bluesy G (♭7th) that fit in tidily with the pattern of the descending triplets. His momentum and phrasing carries him quickly and smoothly into measure 15 over the G7 chord, where triplets and eighth-note pull-offs in the G major scale, with the addition of the funky C♯ (♯4th), finally awards him the checkered flag in measure 16 over the A chord via an open-position A5 voicing.

Performance Tip: In measure 9, bend the B note on string 1 with the ring finger while holding down the E on string 2 with the index finger. The B string gets muted by the bent E string, but this still allows for a quick double-stop to happen on beat 1.

Fig. 18

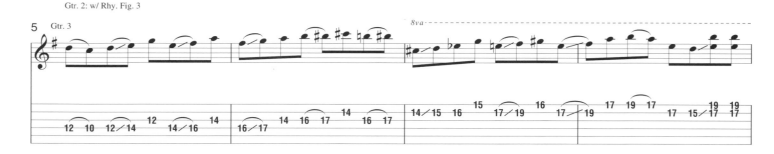

MUD ON THE TIRES

(*Mud on the Tires*, 2003)
Words and Music by Brad Paisley and Chris DuBois

The title track of his third release hit #30 on the *Billboard* Hot 100, and guitarist Redd Volkaert added extra six-string muscle to several album tracks as Paisley started to expand his audience beyond his core of loyal country music fans. As is often realized, his lyrics contain a little sly innuendo and metaphors beneath the seeming innocence of his country romance tale.

Figure 19—Intro

(NOTE: Fret positions will refer to the tab even though the actual pitches sound two frets higher due to the capo.)

Though extravagantly and inordinately praised for his incendiary electric solos, Paisley is a complete guitarist. The intro is a fine example of the way he (Gtr. 1) blends acoustic arpeggios, partial chords, and double stops into an unbroken "string" of musical ideas. Observe how he plays the lowest bass note on the downbeat of each chord change, which creates a descending line from C (C), B (G/B), A (Am), G (C/G), and F (Fadd9) through measure 3, after which he ends with "uplift" in measure 4 provided by the G note and chord. More importantly, be sure to hear how Paisley employs subtle chord melody to preview the vocal melody of the verse that contains virtually the same progression. In addition, pay attention to the hammer-ons that also contribute variety to the phrasing.

Performance Tip: As notated, either use a thumbpick and bare fingers or "hybrid picking," like Paisley, which involves the flatpick held between the thumb and index fingers along with the middle and ring fingers. The general approach would be to utilize the pick for strings 6–4 and the bare fingers on strings 3–1.

Fig. 19

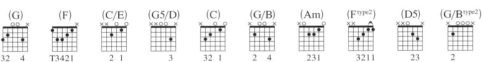

Gtr. 1: Capo II

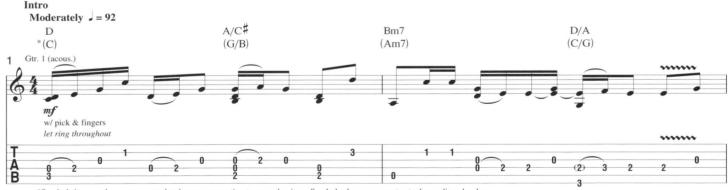

*Symbols in parentheses represent chord names respective to capoed guitars. Symbols above represent actual sounding chords.
Capoed fret is "0" in tab. Chord symbols reflect overall harmony.

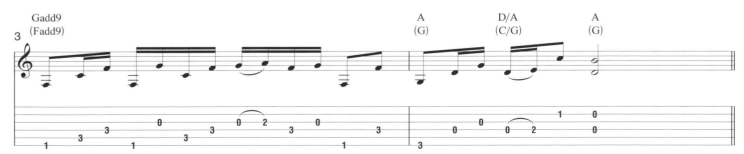

Figure 20—Verse 2

(NOTE: Gtr. 2 is not capoed and is transcribed playing pitches relative to D, the actual key.)

By verse 2, Paisley (Gtr. 2) is fast at work displaying another aspect of his instrumental skills by filling tastefully around his vocals. This time out, his scale of choice is the D major scale over the four-measure progression of D (I)–A/C# (V), Bm (vi)–D/A, G (IV), and D–A that is repeated twice for a total of eight measures. Be sure to see how he follows every chord change with the appropriate *target note*, be it the 3rd (C# over A/C#) or root (A bent to B over Bm, D over D/A, G over G, D over D, F# bent to G over G, and D over D in measure 5).

Equally important, however, is the other part of the soloing equation consisting of his phrasing. Paisley is a master of his genre and, in the relatively short span of time, plays something entirely different in each measure. As is often his custom, he enters with squawking chicken pickin' on the bass strings in measure 1 over the A/C# change. He then slips right into a one-step bend from E to F# that is sustained over both the Bm and D/A chords for most of measure 2, making the time feel more elastic, until he ends on E pulled of to the open 4th (D) string. Remaining low in the bass register, Paisley pulls and hammers notes related to the G harmony including the open third (G) and fourth strings for some Tele twang before making like a pedal steeler in measure 4 over the A change. Check out the addition of the G# on beat 1 that is not naturally in the D major scale, but is the major 7th of A, making for a very "inside" sound as well as functioning as the "leading tone" to "lead" the ear into the measure. The bent G (b7th) released to F# (6th) that follows with the E (5th) bent to F# and released back to E creates a wobbly "steel" effect that again is in dynamic contrast to what has gone and will come, where perfect resolution arrives in measure 5 with a sustained D (root) note. The overall concept should be seen as a fluid, graceful sequence of ascending and descending licks that complement the wistful, romantic nature of the lyrics.

Performance Tip: In measure 4, play the G# with the index finger, bend the F# with the ring finger, and bend the E with the index finger. The latter may take some extra muscle, depending on string gauge.

39 Full Band

40 Slow Demo
Gtr. 1   meas. 1–4

Fig. 20

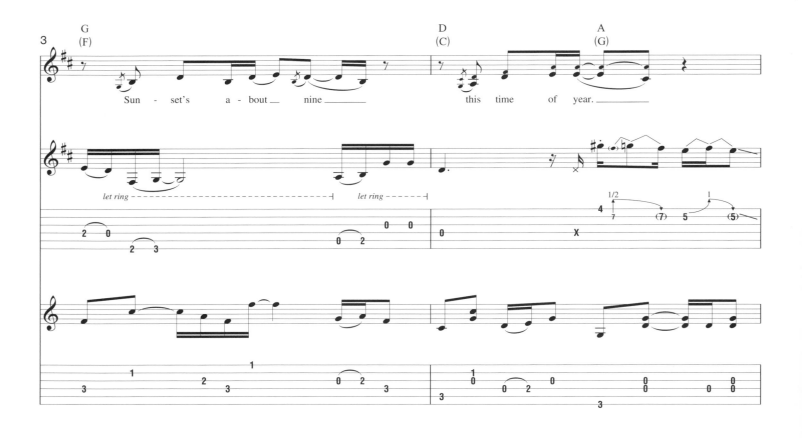

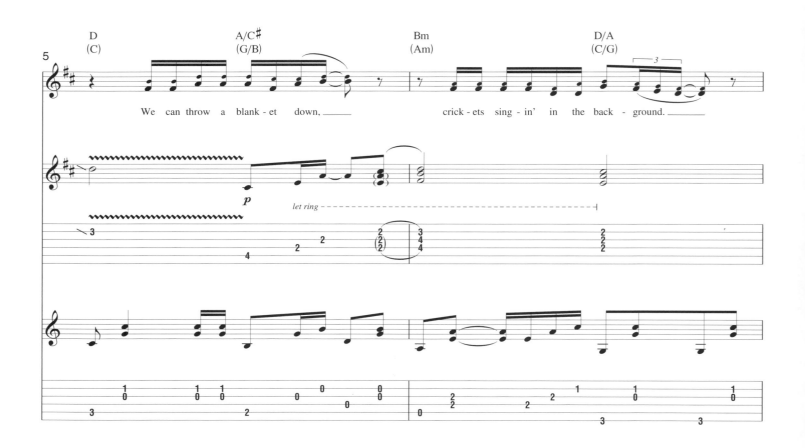

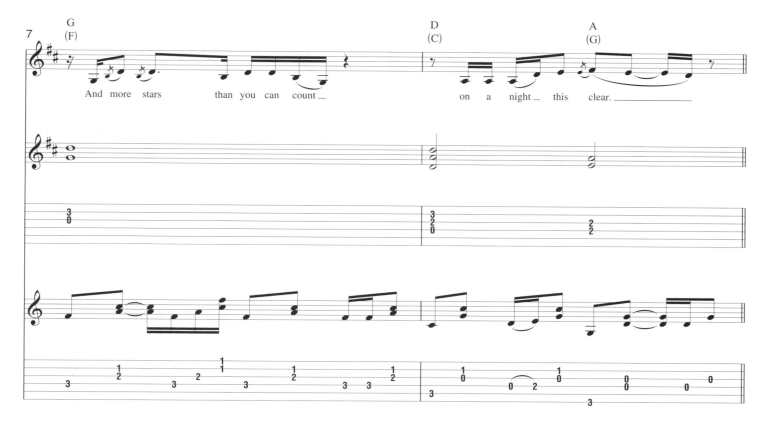

Figure 21—Outro Guitar Solo

After taking it nice and easy up to this point in the song, Paisley (Gtr. 2) decides to go out with power and passion for the 13-measure outro solo. Measures 1–10 consist of A (V), G (IV), A, G–D/F♯ (I)–A5/E–D, A, D–A/C♯, Bm, D, A, G, and A. Measures 11–13 finish things up with G, G–D/F♯–E5–A/C♯, and D in a free-time ritard.

Paisley once again uses the D major scale for his main improvisational "tool" as he did in the verses and, once again, makes an auspicious entrance on the bass strings with a behind-the-nut bend of D (4th) to E (5th) on string 4 over the A change. Radically shifting his tack for dynamic purposes, he chicken picks string 6 in measure 2 over the G chord, muting and scratching percussively while repeatedly banging on the G (root) note. In measures 3, 4, and 5 over the A, G–D/F♯–A5/E–D, and A changes, he sprints up, down, and up the scale with stuttering sextuplets and thirty-second notes, boosting the forward momentum of the solo with great gusto while adding variety to the phrasing. Amazingly, even within the flood of notes, Paisley is able to emphasize every chord change, including the IV in measure 4, with choice chord tones. Highlights are C♯/A (3rd/root) in measure 3 and D/B (5th/3rd of G), D (root of D), E (5th of A5/E), and D and F♯ (root and 3rd of D) in measure 4.

Coming out of measure 5 into measure 6 over the D and A/C♯ chords, Paisley relaxes the tightly coiled musical tension by sustaining the A (5th of D) and following with the A (root) and E (5th) notes over the A/C♯ change. Dynamically, he drops to the low B (root) on string 5 in measure 7 over the Bm chord and "strums" a Bm7 triple stop and hip dyad of E/B (9th/root) to suggest a jazzy Bm9 for extra harmony. Maintaining the concept into measure 8 over the D chord with additional relaxed phrasing, Paisley utilizes A/E (5th/9th) and the E bent to F♯ (3rd) along with a chromatic run of F♯–F (♭3rd)–E that relates directly to the D harmony. Observe the F♯ (bent courtesy of his G-bender) that sustains over top of the chromatic notes for a rich, pedal steel effect. In measures 9 over the A chord, he employs wide interval leaps for more dynamic hijinks, in addition to bending the B (2nd) to C♯ (3rd) to help define the major tonality. He next twists down the D major scale in measure 10 over the G and A changes, making sure to nip the G (root), A (root), and C♯ (3rd) notes along the way to measure 11 where he bends the F♯ (major 7th) one-half step to G (root) for satisfying resolution.

But wait, there's more! In measure 12 over the G–D/F#–E5–A/C# changes, Paisley starts with a G major triad and creates a beautiful, descending melodic line that resolves with finality to D (root) over the D chord via a half-step bend up from C#.

Performance Tip: The bend of the E in measure 8 with corresponding harmony notes is virtually impossible without a G-bender. However, the ones on the bass strings in measures 1, 11, and 13 should be executed by pulling *down* with the ring finger or middle finger.

41 **Full Band**

42 **Slow Demo**
Gtr. 2   meas. 1–11

Fig. 21

Outro Guitar Solo

Double-time feel

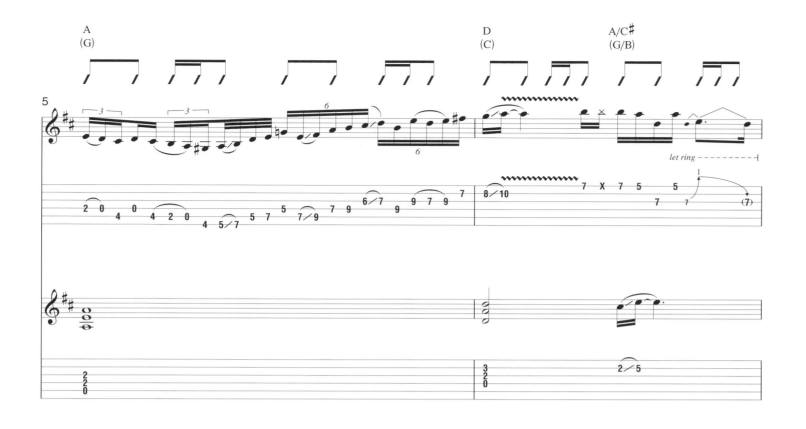

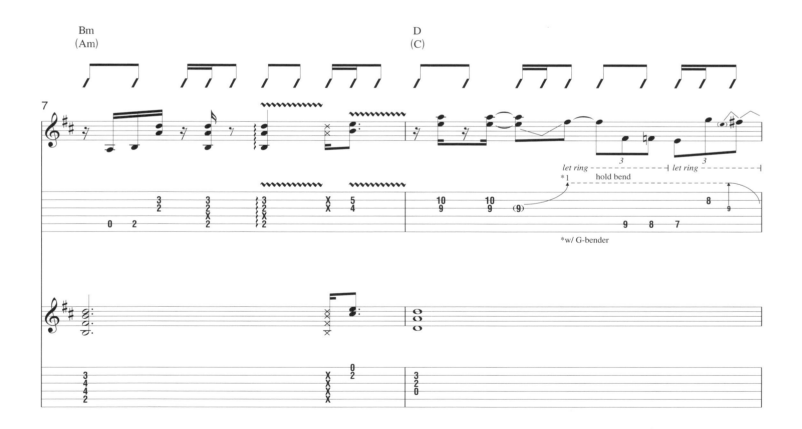

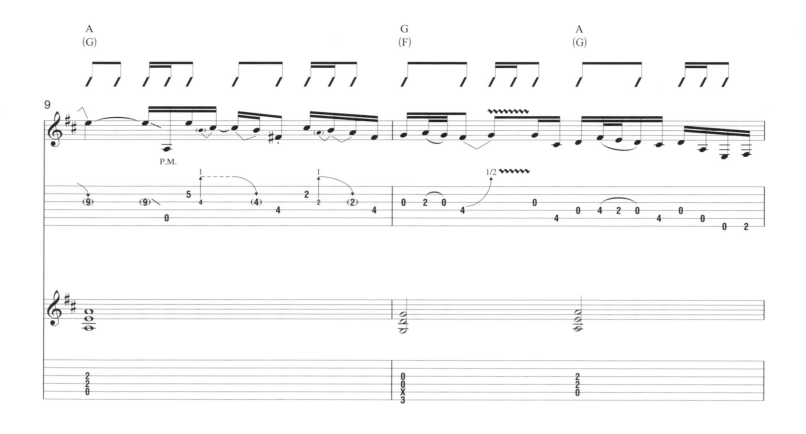

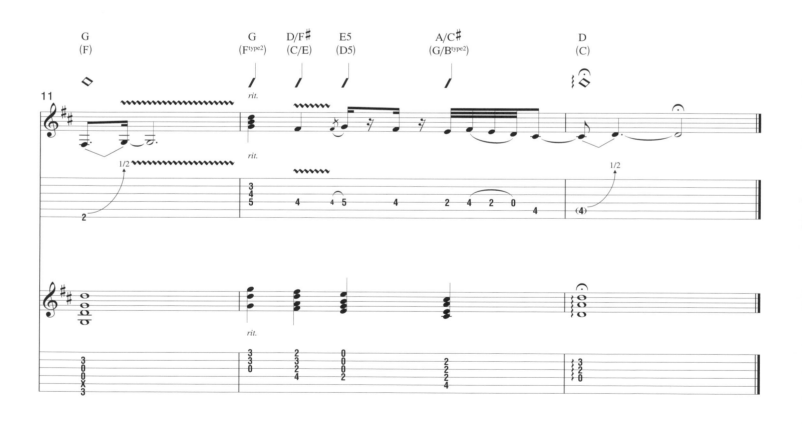

THE NERVOUS BREAKDOWN

(*Who Needs Pictures*, 1999)

Words and Music by Brad Paisley, James Gregory and Mitch McMichen

The picture of him on the cover of his debut CD wearing a black hat is visual indication that Paisley would have a few more releases to go to find his image with the "good guy" white hat. Likewise, he had not yet found his true "voice" as a skillful, clever songwriter. However, the hot instrumental blast of "The Nervous Breakdown" was a figurative "warning shot" fired across the bow of swaggering country pickers everywhere.

Figure 22—Section A

Measures 1–8 of section A function as a de facto intro. Paisley uses bluegrass-type flatpicking licks derived from the G composite blues scale (Mixolydian mode plus blues scale) in the root-octave position to create a heart-thumping and memorable "head" that he next elaborates on and embellishes. Check out that since Paisley (Gtr. 1) is playing unaccompanied licks, the harmony could be seen to be implied as indicated with G (I), C (IV), and D (V) changes. In addition, be aware that he is playing acoustic instead of electric guitar, requiring extra hand strength and accuracy in order to articulate cleanly.

Performance Tip: Virtually all the licks in measures 1–4 may be played with just the ring and index fingers. The pull-offs in measures 5 and 6, however, should be accessed as follows: Place the index and ring fingers on the A and D notes, low to high. Use the middle finger to play the B♭ on string 3 at fret 3. Pull off to the index and open third string, followed by playing the F note on string 4 with the middle finger.

Fig. 22

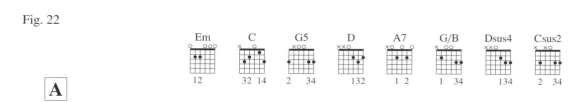

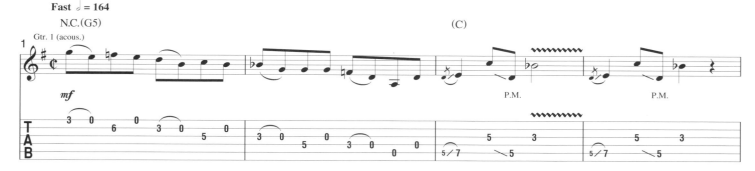

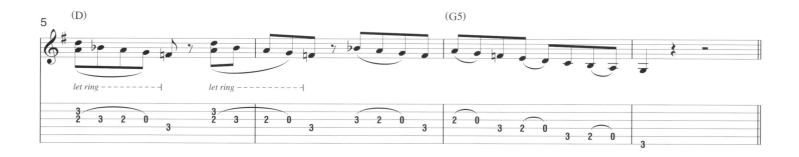

Figure 23—Section C

If section A is accepted as the "head" of the tune, then section C should be appreciated as the secondary theme or melody. It is so strong that it could easily stand on its own as the main theme or "head," and its sparse simplicity stands in stark dynamic contrast to literally all of the other sections. Adding substance is the harmony played in unison with Paisley by the various other instruments for a deep, rich sound. The 32-measure progression is composed of four eight-measure sections. The changes in measures 1–8 are Em (vi), Em, Em, Em, C (IV), C, G5 (I), and G5. Measures 9–16 contain Em, Em, Em, Em, C, C, D (V), and D chords, 17–24 contain exactly the same harmonic changes as 1–8, and 25–32 consist of A7 (II), A7, A7, A7–G/B, C, C, D–Dsus4, and D chords.

In measures 1–4, Paisley (Gtr. 3) combines a decidedly non-country, single-note, eighties "arena rock" melody fashioned from the G major scale with big, sustained C and G5 chords in measures 5–8. In measures 9–12, he repeats the anthemic melody from measures 1–4 while creating a new, but related, melodic line for measures 13–16 over the C and D changes, respectively. Measures 17–20 likewise feature the same melodic line as 1–4 and 9–12, but measures 21–24, instead of utilizing the same sustained chord voicings of 5–8, present yet another melodic line with considerable breathing space around it for dynamic contrast.

Using the subtle musical tension accrued through the repetition in the previous sections as a springboard, in measures 25–32, Paisley takes full advantage of the uplift provided by the chord changes that begin a 4th higher in measures 25–28. With the same unerring ear for the right choice of notes as he previously displayed, he invents another catchy line over the A7, G/B, C, and D chords. If anything, the melody is even sweeter than what preceded by virtue of fewer instruments adding their harmony "voices" thereby allowing the warm tone of the guitar to shine through brightly in the climax of the section.

Performance Tip: Play the bend in measure 11 by pulling *down* with the index finger as if utilizing a hook.

45 Full Band

46 Slow Demo
Gtr. 3   meas. 25–32

Fig. 23

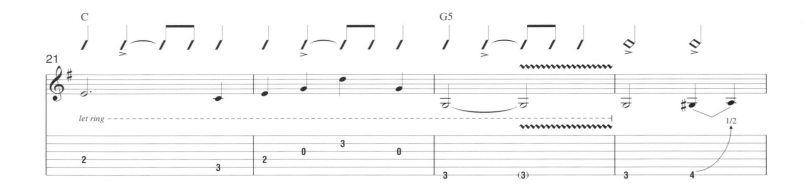

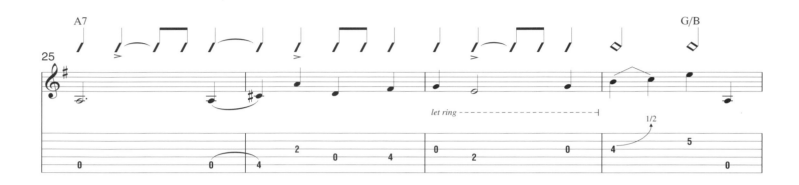

Figure 24—Section D

Section D is similar to section B (not shown), but it repeats as the main theme of the song and is actually derived from an expanded, electric version of section A. Measures 1–16 are comprised of the same chord changes as the same measures of section B: G5 (I), G5, Csus2 (IV), Csus2, G5, G5, D (V), D, G5, G5, Csus2, Csus2, G5, D, G5, and G5. The additional measures of 17–19 contain sustained G, Gsus4, and G5add#4 chords, one per measure, as a transition to section E (Fig. 26).

Also, similar to sections A and B, the single-note licks are drawn from the G composite blues scale. Notice how the F (♭7th of G) and B♭ (♭7th of C) notes contribute a bluesy vibe, even though the former goes by in a flash for the G change. For the Csus2 chord in measures 3, 4, 11, and 12, however, Paisley (Gtr. 3) sustains and vibratos the B♭ for dynamic contrast against all the fast-fingered notes. The other dynamic exception takes place in measure 8 over the D chord where he sustains and vibratos the C (♭7th) for three relatively long beats. Be aware of how important these details of phrasing can be in a song made up from tons of fleeting eighth notes!

As if more proof was needed, check out measures 7 and 14 over the D chord to better understand the brilliance of Paisley's note selection. In the former, he restricts his palette to the F# (major 3rd), D (root), C# (major 7th), C (♭7th), and E (2nd) notes, all of which, except for the C#, are contained in both the G and D Mixolydian modes. The result makes for a very "inside" sound, as well as helping to establish the tonality of the initial chord changes in measures 1–8. In the latter, however, the D chord just happens to occur in the progression of one-measure chord changes leading to resolution in measure 16 on the G5, and Paisley fires through the measure with the D (root), F (♭3rd),C# (major 7th), C (♭7th), G (4th), B♭ (♭6th), and B (6th) notes. With the G composite blues scale, Paisley maintains continuity with the previous measures employing it to ensure a fast, smooth, and relentless run-down to the conclusion of the section in measure 16.

Performance Tip: Play the hip chords in measure 17–19 as follows: Begin on the G major triad with the ring and middle fingers and the index finger barring strings 2 and 1, low to high, add the pinky on string 3 at fret 5 for the Gsus4, then move it up to fret 6 for the G5add#4.

Fig. 24

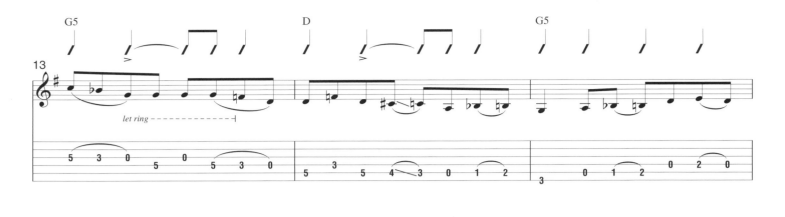

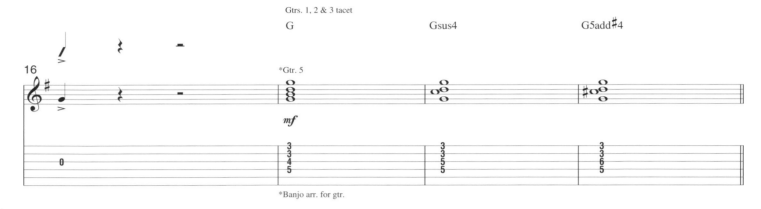

*Banjo arr. for gtr.

Figure 25—Section E

Chomping at the bit to cut loose, Paisley (Gtr. 3) finally takes an improvised solo in the 32 measures of section E that certainly serve to highlight the title of "The Nervous Breakdown." It is composed of four eight-measure progressions heard throughout the track consisting of G5 (I), G5, Csus2 (IV), Csus2, G5, G5, D (V), and D in both measures 1–8 and 17–24 with basically the same changes in measures 9–16 and 25–32 except that the last three measures of each section are D, G5, and G5.

Paisley logically and intelligently approaches his solo in eight-measure chunks with the G composite blues scale. Measures 1 and 2 of the first installment begin with a hint of traditional Bakersfield honky-tonk phrasing as he nails the G tonality by bending the A (2nd) to B (3rd) followed by the D (5th) and the open third (G) string for the root. From there, it is "off to the races" as he flatpicks like a demon in the scale's open position until he arrives at the D change in measures 7–8. There he executes an ascending chromatic line on string 5 (actually beginning on the root note in measure 6) of D#–E–F–F# with each note alternating with its 3rd (F#–G–G#–A) on string 4. Resolution is achieved in measure 8 on the D (root) on string 3 at fret 7. The purpose of the pattern is threefold: One, it provides extra propulsion to a solo that is already plowing ahead with unbound exuberance; two, it draws attention to the chord change; and three, it makes for a definite demarcation as the end of these eight measures.

Measures 9–16 are neatly subdivided into two four-measure sections, the first of which starts with a descending run that begins on string 2 at fret 6 (F) and ends on string 5 at fret 3 (C). Measures 13–16 commence on the open fifth (A) string ascending to conclusion on string 2 at fret 8 (G). Also contributing to the "ebb and flow" are alternating "waves" of tension and release. See that measures 9–10 over the G5 chord do not contain the root or 3rd thereby creating musical tension to jumpstart the proceedings that is quickly released in measures 11–12 over the Csus2 changes with repetition on the C (root) note. Likewise, neither measure 13 over the G5 chord nor measure 14 over the D chord contain the root, resulting in another dose of tension that is then released in measures 15–16 over the G5 change with solid resolution to G (root).

In the next eight-measure section, Paisley opts for a completely different change of improvisational direction by repeating a similar lick phrased with "country swing" in measures 17–22. It consists of the chord tones of B (3rd), D (5th), and G (root) over G5 in measures 17, 18, 21, and 22 and C (root), D (2nd), and G (5th) over Csus2 in measures 19 and 20. The sharp focus on the tightly coiled lick offers welcome dynamic contrast to the long lines of eighth notes that make up most of the solo. Additionally, do not miss the way Paisley breaks the pattern in measures 23 and 24 over the D chord, creating more tension with notes from the G composite blues scale, that skirts around the D tonality in the former except for the F♯ (3rd) that speeds on by. However, he smartly sustains the A (5th) for three beats in the latter and then cleverly inserts the open third (G) string on beat 4 over the G5 played as anticipation to the next section.

After firmly establishing the G tonality with the D (5th) and B (3rd) notes in measure 25 of the climactic last eight measures, Paisley tears into a group of similar pull-off licks in measures 26–29 that produces much more tension and forward momentum than those in measures 17–22. Quite simply, it is the result of his quicksilver execution and the tension of the F note, functioning as the ♭7th of G and the 4th of C, that brings the solo to a climactic conclusion with a few surprises. For example, in measure 30 over the D chord, he utilizes the fingering for an open position D major triad combined with the open fourth (D) and third (G) strings for a brief, dynamic dollop of texture and harmony. In measure 31 over the G change, he dynamically leaps above the octave at fret 12 on string 4, including the huge interval of the open third and second (B) strings to the fretted F (♭7th) at fret 15 on string 4. With the open fourth and third strings in measure 32 and the startling, sweeping gliss down the neck from the B at fret 19 on string 6, the two measures end with a bang.

Performance Tip: In measures 1 and 2, bend the A note with the middle finger backed up by the index finger and access the D note with the ring finger.

Fig. 25

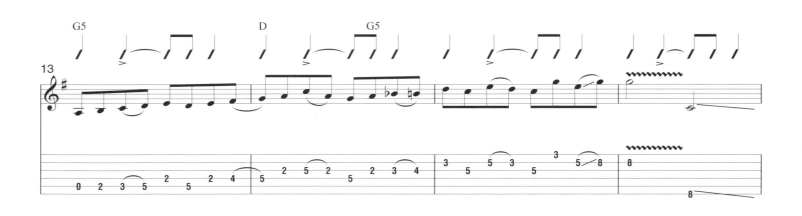

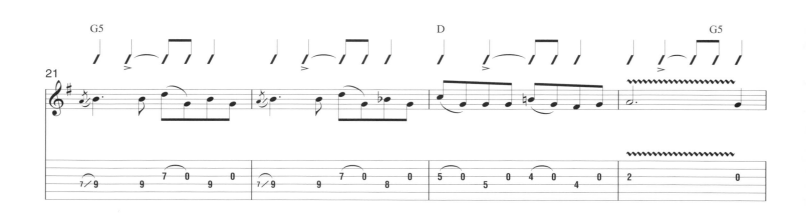

ONLINE

(*5th Gear*, 2007)
Words and Music by Brad Paisley, Chris DuBois and Kelley Lovelace

Paisley would be considered a first-rate composer of creative, well-crafted songs that often address contemporary topics with satirical humor and cynical insights, even if he worked in the rock and pop genres. The fact that he has chosen to indulge his wide-ranging observations in the traditionally-conservative world of country music about D–I–V–O–R–C–E and pickup trucks is all the more impressive. With gentle sarcasm that contains enough barbs to give his song bite, he skewers the fantasy perpetrated in online chat rooms. Figuratively, if not literally composed to cross over, the single made it to #39 on the *Billboard* Top 100 charts.

Figure 26—Intro

After four measures of organ chords implying Gsus4–G5, Gsus4, G5, and Gsus4–F5, Paisley (Gtr. 1) enters in his pedal steel guise for the next eight measures—essentially a I–IV (G–C) vamp with an F5 (♭VII) added every four measures. Notice that measures 5, 7, 9, and 11 of G–G7 changes contain the same pattern, as do measures 6, 8, and 10 for the C chord. Only measure 12 (C) deviates as a way of producing a logical and definite end to the intro as well as providing a smooth transition to the G5 chord in measure 1 of the verse (not shown). The ringing G–G7 riffs contain broken open-position chords that are picked high to low. The twisted C riffs are dynamically more propulsive as Paisley creatively hammers to E (3rd) from the open fourth (D) and third (G) strings, with resolution to the C (root) note.

Performance Tip: For the G riffs, pick with downstrokes for the fretted G, F, and C notes. Use upstrokes for the D, G (open third string), and D notes.

Fig. 26

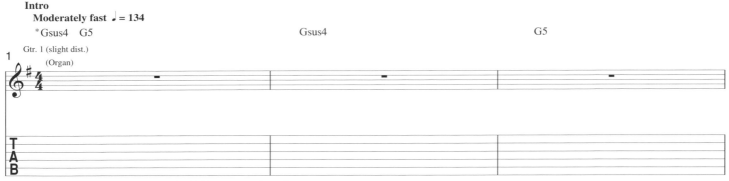

*Chord symbols reflect basic harmony (implied by organ, next 4 meas.).

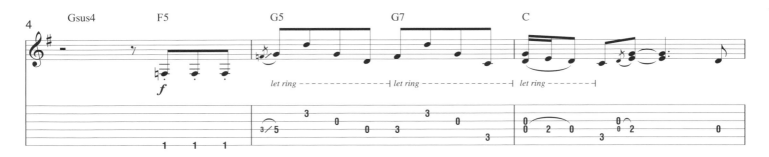

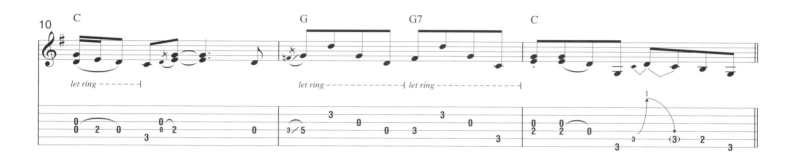

Figure 27—Violin/Guitar Solo

The eight-measure solo is actually a duet between fiddler Aubrey Haynie (arranged as Gtr. 2) and Paisley (Gtr. 1), with Haynie's whiplash lines transcribed for guitar. Consequently, it is worthwhile to distinguish between the two parts and mention that even one passage played by Haynie would seem a frightening challenge for most guitarists, including Paisley and his super chops.

Haynie opens the "competition" in measures 1 and 2 over the Em (vi)–D (V) and C (IV) changes with surprisingly cool blues licks derived from the E minor pentatonic scale (here tabbed in the root-octave position at fret 12). Check out the blues-approved "bend" of D (♭7th) to E (root) in measure 1 and the startling guitar-like licks in measure 2, like the "bend" from A (6th) to B (major 7th), that are staples of blues-rockers everywhere. Meanwhile, Paisley bides his time with big, open-position chord voicings before easing into his space in measures 3–4 with choice E (3rd) and G (5th) notes preceding the A (6th) bent across the bar line where it arrives at B (3rd) over the G (I) in measure 3. Letting Haynie take the "high road" while taking the "low road," Paisley duplicates the licks from measure 2 in the open-position of the G major pentatonic scale. Observe that the bend from A (2nd) to B (3rd) over the G change in measure 3 also functions in complementing the major tonality. In measure 4 over the D chord, however, he emphasizes the D (root) note with fretted notes and the open fourth string.

In measures 5 and 6 over the Em and C chords, respectively, Haynie "challenges" Paisley by flying in with a blur of thirty-second notes from the E Aeolian mode. A virtuosic display of serpentine phrasing and smart note selection, the Herculean run begins on the bass strings with D (♭7th) and E (root) notes and ends in measure 6 with a "bend" of A (6th) to the sweet B (major 7th) in the upper register. At the same time, Paisley "goofs off" in measure 5 by plucking the open sixth (E) string and pushes forward on the neck of his axe to lower the pitch a funky half step, followed by a hammer-on from F♯ (2nd) to G (♭3rd) to help define the Em tonality.

Astoundingly, in measures 7 and 8 over G and D changes, Paisley nearly matches Haynie's prodigious output. See how he comes back at the fiddling "fool" with a fret-melting run from the open fifth (A) string across the fretboard in the G major scale that peaks at the G (4th) on beat 1 over the D change and descends back to the open fifth string. Be aware that the C♯ (♯4th) on beat 4 of measure 7 and beat 1 of measure 8 serves as a passing tone between C and D while not theoretically in the G major scale. Though Paisley does not play as many thirty-second notes as Haynie, the sextuplets are a dizzying display of his virtuosity.

Performance Tip: Execute the repeating licks in measure 3 by pulling off from the D note on string 2 with the ring finger to the open second string and bending the A note on string 3 with the middle finger.

53 Full Band

54 Slow Demo
Gtr. 1   meas. 3–4,
          7–8

Fig. 27

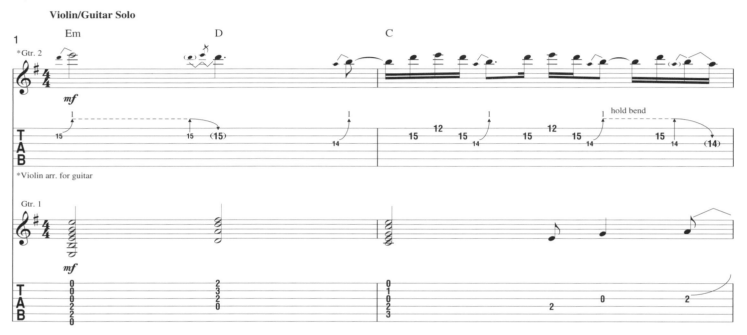

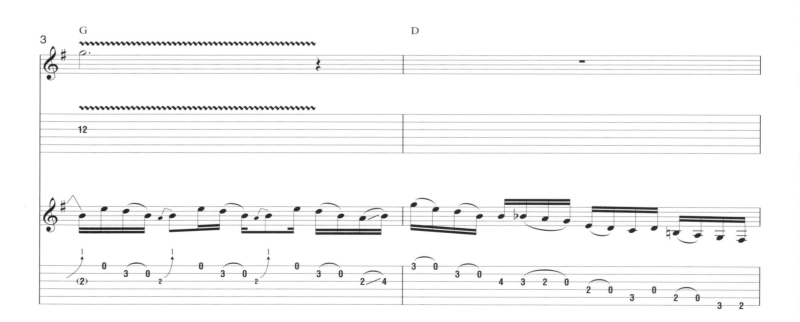

ONLINE

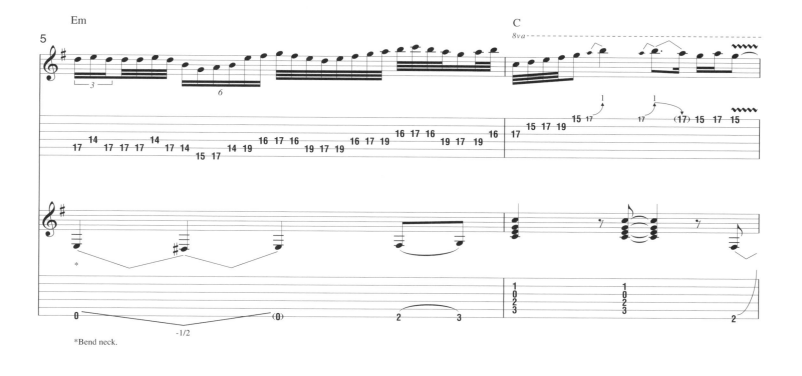

*Bend neck.

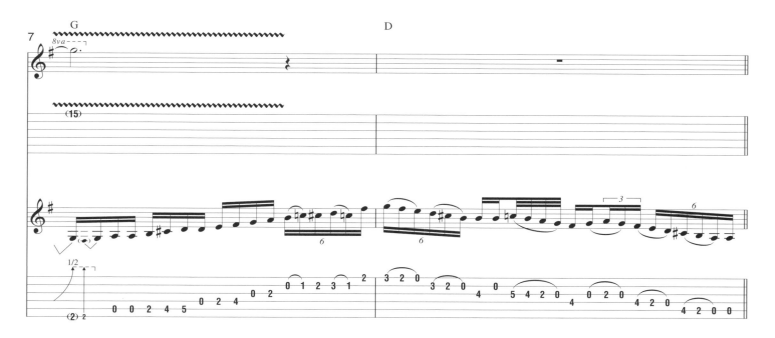

Figure 28—Guitar Solo

Over an essentially I–IV, two-measure vamp of G (I)–F ($\flat$VII) and C (IV) that repeats for 20 measures (including two extra of G tacked on for a total of 22), Paisley (Gtr. 1) figuratively lets out the pent-up frustration of his protagonist in "Online" with a wild assortment of licks from the G major scale. In measures 1–8, he runs around in his most comfortable locale of the open position where he can insert twanging open strings to his heart's content. Check out how he manages to nick the root notes of each chord in every measure to maintain a sense of logic and structure, though he does save his longest and fastest runs for measures 6 and 8 that just contain the C chord, allowing him to stretch-out further.

In measures 9–14, Paisley begins to branch out in terms of his scale positions and techniques as he slowly builds momentum towards conclusion in measure 21. Notice the slightly dissonant, bluesy double-string bends of a quarter step in measures 9 and 10, for example, that rivet musical tension and provide dynamic contrast to the long, sizzling lines more typical of the solo as in measures 11 and 12. Likewise, in measures 13 and 14, Paisley dynamically drops down to the bass strings and even bends the neck of his Tele (NOTE: *Do not try this with a prized axe!*) to raise the open sixth (E) string by one-half step to F (root) of the F (♭VII) chord on beat 3 of measure 13.

Measures 15 and 16 contain the initial climax of the solo as Paisley whips on up to the root-octave position of the E minor pentatonic scale (functioning as the G major pentatonic scale, or *relative minor scale*, of G in the world of Nashville guitar) at fret 12. He bends the D (6th) one step to E (major 7th) over the F chord in measure 15 for solid consonance, but then cranks it up one-and-one-half steps to F (4th) over the C (IV) in measure 16. The resulting musical tension, greatly enhanced by his stuttering, repeating bend, is startling, to say the least, compared to the harmonious and melodic major scale lines that preceded it and it is the figurative and literal high point of the solo. As one would hope, Paisley releases the aggressive tension in measure 17 over the G (I) and F changes by sustaining and vibratoing the B (3rd) on string 2 at fret 12 for the former and, for the latter, playing notes from lower positions of the G major pentatonic scale that correspond to F, including C (5th) and D/A (6th/3rd) with the open fourth and fifth strings.

Paisley continues to keep his licks close to the harmony of the chord changes of C and G–F in measures 18 and 19, respectively. He anchors the C chord with E/C/G (3rd/root/5th), the G with the open D (5th) and G (root) strings, and the F change with C/F (5th/root) and its inversion. Along with the relatively relaxed phrasing that gradually increases in intensity, it presents a dynamic foil for the skipping and tumbling notes from the C major scale that follow in measure 20 over the C changes. The result makes for a last rush of adrenalin, like an electric shock, just before Paisley resolves with finality via a gliss down the neck from G/D (root/5th) at fret 12 on beat 1 of the G chord in measure 21.

55 Full Band

56 Slow Demo
Gtr. 1   meas. 6–12,
18–20

Fig. 28

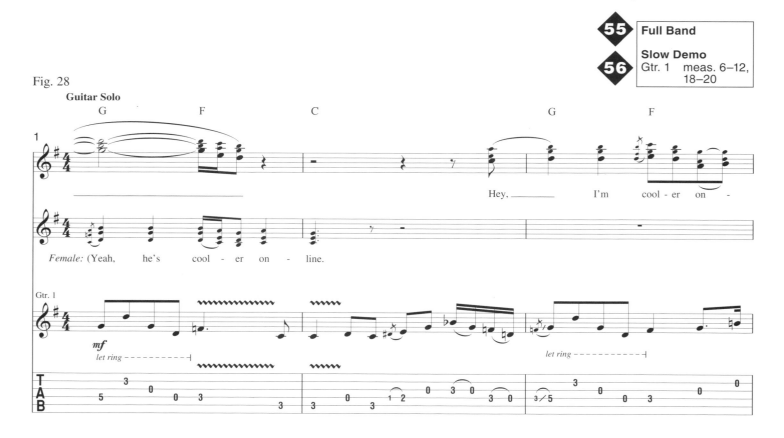

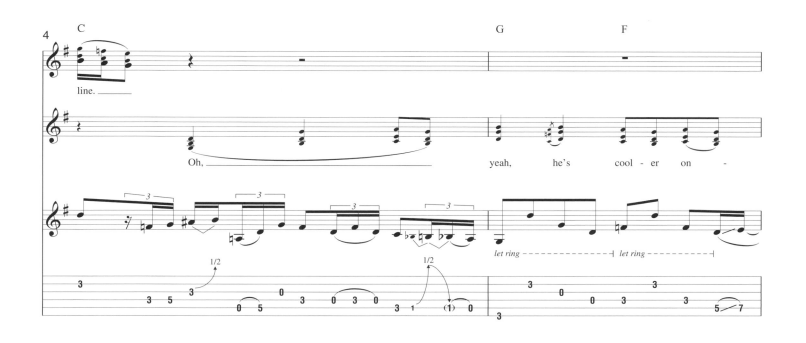

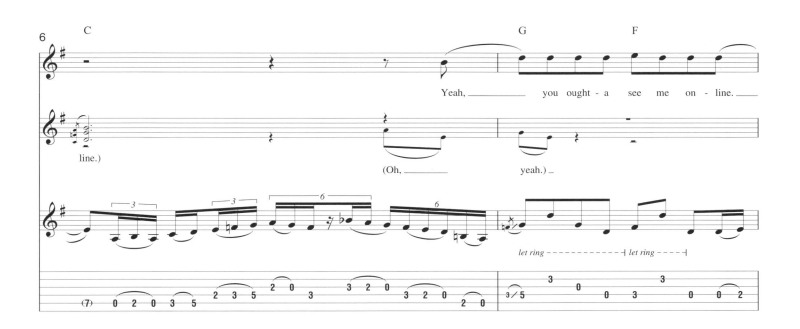

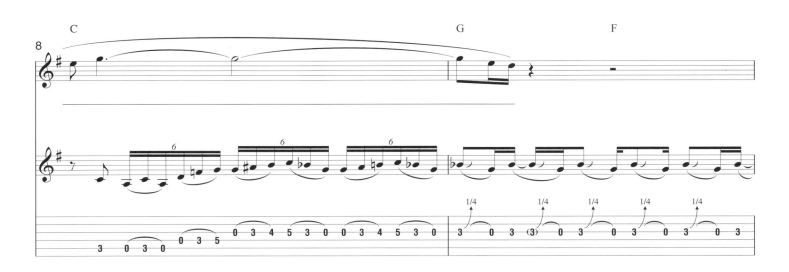

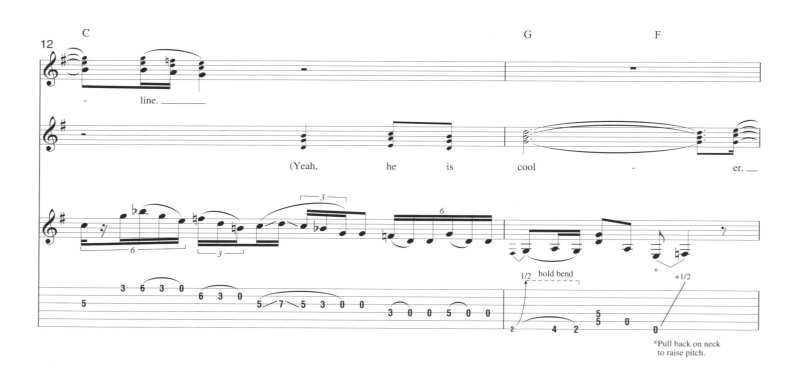

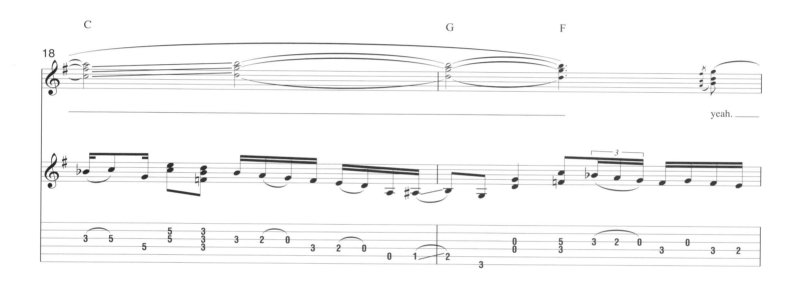

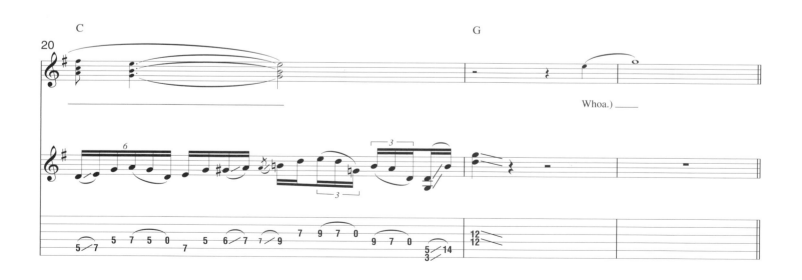

START A BAND

(*Play: The Guitar Album*, 2008)
Words and Music by Kelley Lovelace, Ashley Gorley and Dallas Davidson

When the opportunity finally arrived for Paisley and his close friend Keith Urban to cut a track together, Paisley was determined, "…that the end result would be more than just two entertainers playing together." He wanted something, "…really cool that people are going to talk about and want to hear… not a blazing fast thing… more of a rockin' Eagles-style tune, like back when Joe Walsh and Don Felder would play those harmony parts." Originally written for *Time Well Wasted*, "Start a Band" has lyrics that both musicians could relate to along with countless other would-be rock stars.

Figure 29—Intro

The nine-measure progression of the intro also appears in the interlude (not shown) that contains F5 (I), B♭5 (IV), C5 (V), D5 (vi), F5, B♭5, C5–B♭5, F, and F changes. Paisley (Gtr. 1) sets the table in the pickup measure with a saucy melodic lick from the F major pentatonic scale. A bold statement is then made in measure 1 over the F5 change as Paisley executes a classic "country harmony" bend—in an unusual way via the G-bender—resulting in C/A (5th/3rd) to enrich the F major tonality that is resolved on beat 4 with the F (root) note. By the time he arrives at measure 5 over the F chord, Keith Urban (Gtr. 4), who is capoed at fret 1, commences to chip in with tasty, "country-approved" licks in the F major scale. Observe the cool move he makes in measure 6 over the B♭5 chord by playing the B♭ (root) and D (3rd) notes to define the tonality. Meanwhile, Paisley, after doing his duty by accompanying with a B♭5 in measure 6, finishes out the intro by weaving lines in from the F major pentatonic scale around Urban's musings.

57 Full Band

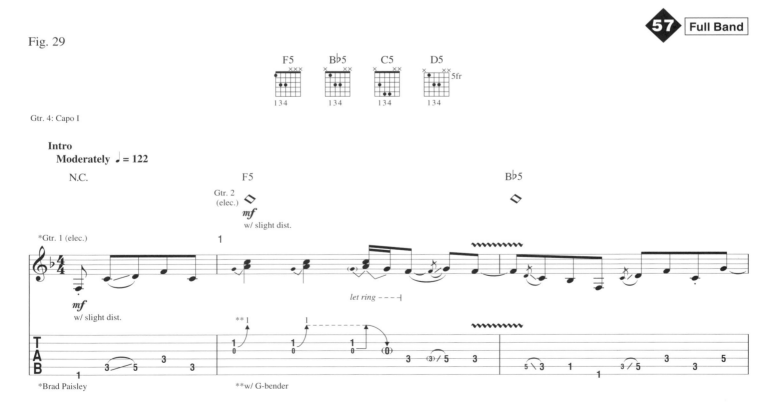

Fig. 29

Gtr. 4: Capo I

Intro
Moderately ♩ = 122

*Gtr. 1 (elec.)

*Brad Paisley   **w/ G-bender

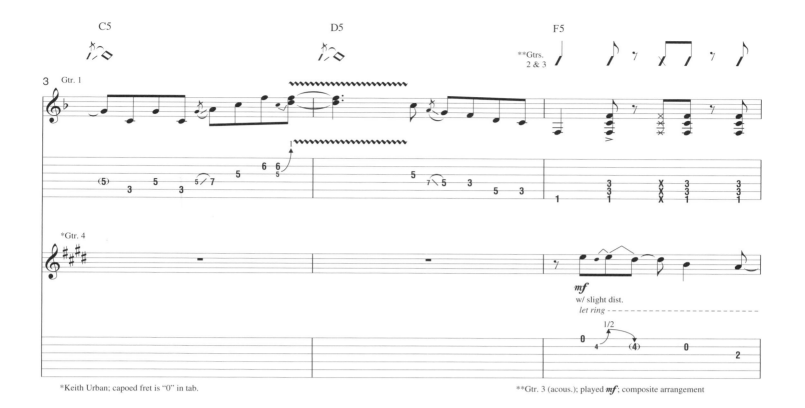

*Keith Urban; capoed fret is "0" in tab.

**Gtr. 3 (acous.); played *mf*; composite arrangement

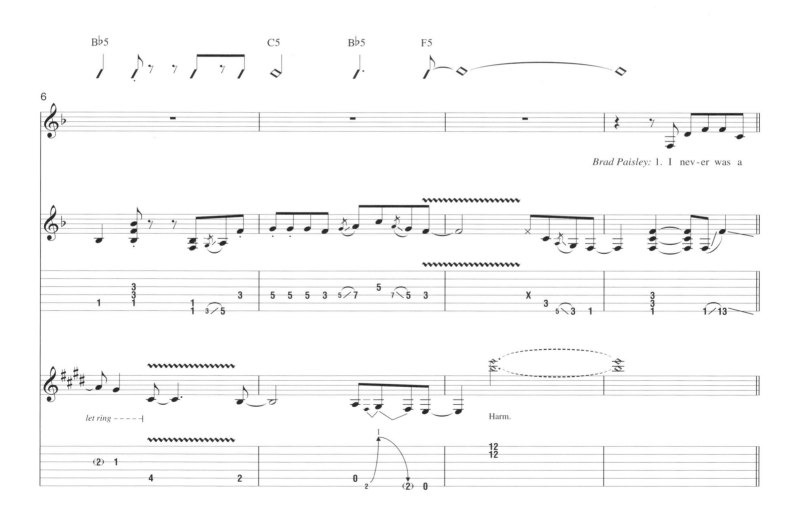

Brad Paisley: 1. I nev-er was a

Figure 30—Verse 2

Urban sings about the popular fantasy of exacting revenge on the girls who snubbed him in high school in the eight measures of verse 2. Meanwhile, his running buddy, Paisley (Gtrs. 1 & 5) comps chords and fills skillfully under and around the vocals over a progression that is the same as the intro minus the last measure of F5 (I). As Gtr. 5, he keeps a rock vibe going by utilizing 5ths as his power chord of choice but only in roughly every other measure (1, 3, 5, 7, and 8). Notice how he voices them all with the root on string 5 as a way of making them fit together smoothly and consistently with the rhythm section.

The reason for Paisley playing chords in every other measure, as Gtr. 5, becomes clear when his role as Gtr. 1 is observed. In the alternate of measure 2, he inserts power chords with the root on string 6, considerably extending the harmony, by moving from A♭5–B5–B♭5 changes that sound suspiciously like "Smoke on the Water!" Then in measure 4, with yet another wink and a nod, he quotes the signature bass-string riff of "Layla" over the D5 change, adding his own interpretation by ending it with A/D/A for a twangy harmony, rather than merely playing the open fourth (D) string. Picking up the pace, he fills measures 5–8 beginning with an F power chord followed by a chimey riff (can you hear the intro to "Sweet Child of Mine?") in F major in measure 6 of the B♭5 change that also intelligently relates to the harmony as the B♭ major pentatonic scale with an added ♭5th (E) note. In measure 7 over the C5 and B♭5 chords, he dynamically opts to just nail the root notes on string 6 and then concludes in measure 8 over the F5 change with a jaunty, soaring, ascending run in the root position of the F major scale that sets up the chorus 2 (not shown).

Performance Tip: Execute the hammer-ons with the middle finger for the "Layla" riff in measure 4.

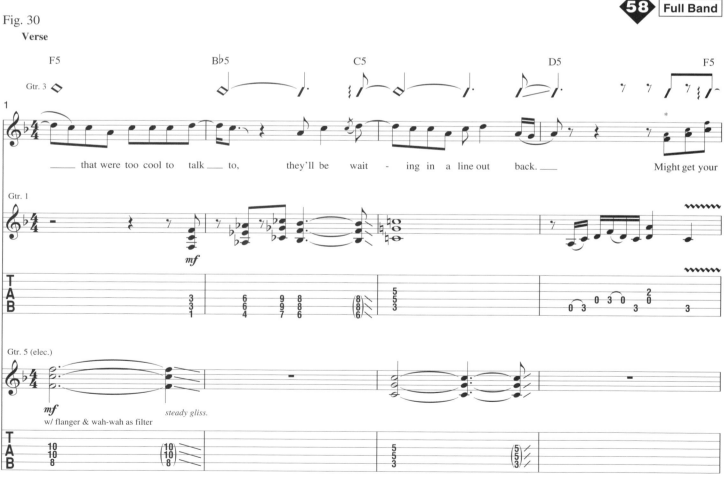

Fig. 30

*Brad Paisley: harmony vocals

Figure 31—Guitar Solo

The 16-measure solo consists of essentially the verse progression in measures 1–8. Measures 9–16 incorporate changes similar to the choruses, however, which contribute to a subtle but unmistakable increase in momentum and anticipation. Check out how the chords are arranged in pairs: C5 (V)–B♭5 (IV) and F5 (I) in measures 9–12, C5–B♭5 and D5 (vi) in measures 13–14, and C5 in measures 15–16.

In measures 1–8, Paisley (Gtr. 1) and Urban (Gtr. 4) more or less trade licks, though 1–4 basically belong to Paisley. In inimitable fashion, he introduces a different technique and approach in each measure. In measure 1 over F5, he uses a classic Keith Richards move by hammering from a C major triad to what implies F/A for a thicker harmony. In measure 2 over B♭5, he slides from the C triad to a B♭ triad and a B♭5 chord at fret 1, smartly utilizing the B♭ (root) note on string 5 to initiate a bass line that walks up to C (root) at fret 3 in measure 3 over the C5 change. Seamlessly transitioning into an arpeggiated open-position C major chord combined with a dynamic, swooping country bend from G (5th) to A (6th) on string 6, Paisley next slips up and into the root position of the D minor pentatonic scale in measure 4 over the D5–C5 changes.

In measures 5–8, Paisley lays back as Urban struts his stuff mainly in the F major pentatonic scale. He begins low on the neck, repeating the honking bend from G to A on string 6 that Paisley employed, then slowly twists his way up the neck to build anticipation. Be sure to see how he cleverly hits the root note of each change even though he remains in the one scale that relates to the key. However, the chords are all in the key of F major, making the technique a logical choice to create structure within the solo. Observe that Urban deviates from his melodic approach in measure 8 over the F5 change with a fluid, imperceptible move from the harmonious F major pentatonic to the root-octave position of the funkier F minor pentatonic scale for a classic blues lick: a slinky bend from G (2nd or 9th) to A (3rd) that returns to G for musical tension. At the same time in measure 8, Paisley dramatically rips his way up through the F major pentatonic scale, voiced in the root position of the D minor pentatonic scale, as a way to encourage forward momentum to measures 9–16 that serve as the highlight of the solo.

Treading a line somewhere between the guitar teams of Joe Walsh/Don Felder and Duane Allman/Dickey Betts, Paisley and Urban let their guitars "sing" together in parallel harmony in measures 9–16. Paisley takes the melody, derived from the D *hexatonic scale* (shades of Dickey Betts!) relative to F major in measures 9–14, and Urban joins in the fun by replicating Paisley's riffs up the neck a 3rd (three or four frets), in the process, automatically creating gorgeous counterpoints. As with their esteemed predecessors, the numerous bends produce a shimmering, vocal-like effect that is particularly affecting and memorable. In measure 15, Paisley leads the way with a descending series of 6ths from C–B♭–A–G–F–E (Mixolydian mode) that begins on beat 4 of measure 14. Urban, however, after responding in kind with 6ths a minor 3rd above for C and B♭, wisely trims down to single notes in 2nds and minor 3rds to not create a logjam of harmony. Both guitarists continue descending with the same approach through beats 1 and 2 of measure 16. The result produces increasingly intense anticipation that is resolved to C (root) on beat 1 of the chorus that follows (not shown), courtesy of a swift, tumbling run down the F major scale with Paisley and Urban in octaves.

Performance Tip: The 6ths should be accessed with the middle and index fingers, low to high.

Fig. 31

59 Full Band

60 Slow Demo
Gtr. 1   meas. 3–4, 8, 15–16
Gtr. 4   meas. 15–16

*Symbols in parentheses represent chord names respective to capoed guitars.
Symbols above reflect actual sounding chords.

Figure 32—Outro

Measures 1–16 of the 23-measure outro contain the eight-measure chord progression of verse 2 repeated two times. Almost eight more measures consisting of two four-measure sections of B♭5 (IV), C5 (V), D5 (vi), F5 (I) and B♭5,C5–B♭5, F5, B♭5 (implied in fade) help propel the progression toward the fade out. This is accomplished due to measures 17 and 21 starting on the B♭ (IV) following the F (I) in measures 16 and 20, instead of repeating the F. Be aware that the chord change from I to IV is the most powerful in terms of forward motion in Western music, hence its extensive usage in blues, R&B, and rock.

Fully delivering on his stated goal of, "creating a song featuring dual guitar lines," Paisley arranges the outro for a virtual parallel harmony guitar sonata in five "movements" that builds in intensity. The "First Movement" occurs in measures 1–8 where Paisley (Gtr. 1) invents "hooky" four-measure melody lines containing lyrical motifs derived from the F major scale that peak in measures 3 and 7 and then resolve and descend gracefully to the F (root) note in measures 4 and 8. Urban (Gtr. 4) actually provides the needed musical tension with harmony lines in major and minor 3rds. They begin to soar with bends, including a beauty of one-and-one-half steps from C (root) to E♭ (♭3rd) played against a Paisley bend from A♭ (♭6th) to B♭ (♭7th) in measure 3 of C5.

The "Second Movement" is contained in measures 9–15 as Paisley changes the "playing field" with descending, arpeggiated triads and triple stops over the F5, B♭5, and C5 chords of measures 9–11 and F5 and B♭5 chords of measures 13–14. Notice the exceedingly hip maneuver in measures 10 and 14 over the B♭5 as Paisley alters the F major first inversion triad of F/C/A (root/5th/3rd), from measures 9 and 13, to F/C/B♭ (5th/2nd/root). In essence, he is "suspending" the 3rd (A) to the 4th (B♭) if analyzed in the key of F. Observe that Urban follows suit by deviating from his triads and triple stops, harmonized in 5ths and 3rds, to include the exact same notes. In addition, check out that both Paisley and Urban insert scalar licks in measures 12 and 15 to incur a "measure" of resolution. In both measures, the former utilizes the root position of the F major pentatonic scale over the D5 change, while the latter works the root-octave position of the F major scale, producing a more random harmony in 3rds, 2nds, and minor 2nds for a break from the predictability of *parallel harmony* (use of the same intervallic distance and movement between two voices).

Measures 16–17 constitute a short "Third Movement" with Paisley using two high-register inversions at fret 17 to accomplish the same effect he created in measures 9–10 and 13–14. This time, however, he employs *second inversion* (5th on bottom) F major triads evolving to an Fsus4 (F–B♭–C) over the F5 and B♭5 chords, respectively. Urban pulls a most surprising lick out of his bag of tricks with the F triad notes of F (root) pulled off to C (5th) followed by A (3rd) in measure 16 and the same pull-off of F (5th) to C (2nd) combined with B♭ (root) in measure 17 to imply the I–IV change for a sparkling and ringing sound that helps to advance the solo. Note the coincidental (?) resemblance to the outro of "Hotel California."

The "Fourth Movement" in measures 18–19 finds Paisley even higher on the fingerboard with C5/D triads over C5 at fret 20 as he reaches the climax of the solo. He follows in measure 19 with an odd harmony of G/F/C (4th/♭3rd/♭7th) at fret 15 over D5 that produces a slightly darker tinge, despite the register, and is a welcome dissonance among all the "sweetness." Urban, meanwhile, also opts to push the envelope with G (5th), D (9th), and C (root) in measure 18 and E (9th), D (root), and A (5th) in measure 19. Be sure to appreciate the vibrancy created by the 9ths in both guitar parts and the harmony in 4ths, 2nds, and 5ths that make for a slice of musical tension as the song begins to quickly fade.

The "Fifth Movement" in measures 20–21 is a virtual repeat of the "Third Movement" in measures 16–17 and is at once a way to herald the end as well as maintain a level of momentum. Measures 22–23, though barely audible in the mix, logically put the capper on the proceedings with Paisley (Gtr. 1) carefully selecting notes from the F major scale that emphasize the C5, B♭5, and F chord changes. Urban utilizes the same scale to provide harmony in 6ths and 3rds. Check out the conclusive resolution over the F5 (I) in measure 23 with Paisley playing the F (root) and Urban the A (3rd), both with fat vibrato. Not content, however, they then combine for a D/F (6th/root) gliss down the neck to produce forward motion to the very end.

Performance Tip: The pull-offs in measures 16–17 and 20–21 of Gtr. 2 (Urban) are a stretch for most guitarists. Clearly, the only practical solution to the technical problem is to use the pinky for the F, the index finger for the C, and the ring finger for the A.

61 Full Band

62 Slow Demo
Gtr. 1   meas. 16–19
Gtr. 4   meas. 16–19

Fig. 32

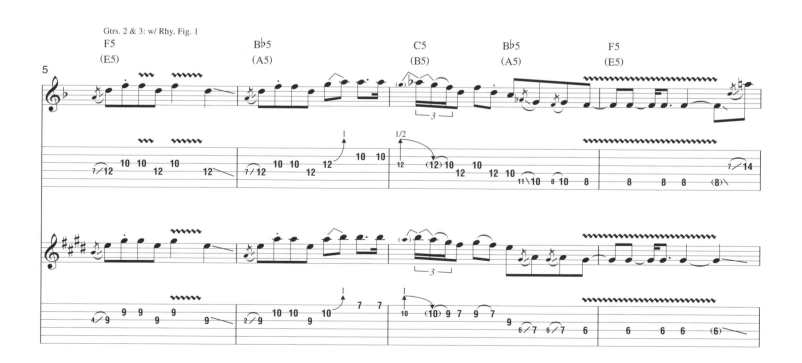

TICKS

(*5th Gear*, 2007)
Words and Music by Brad Paisley, Kelley Lovelace and Tim Owens

"Ticks" not only crossed over, it ran over some boundaries in the process. Besides being #1 on the country charts, it also hit #65 on the Hot Canadian Digital Singles, #34 on the Hot Digital Songs, #48 on the Pop 100, and #40 on the *Billboard* Hot 100. And, though not documented, it likely gave some guys the courage to try a creative new pickup line.

Figure 33—Intro

"Ticks" is arena rock for country fans as Paisley makes a big, bold statement in the stomping, blues-rock of the 11-measure intro. Leading the way as Gtr. 1, he also adds an element of funky syncopation over the E5 (I) chord for five measures with octave E notes as A5 (IV)–E5, B5 (V), A5–E5, C#5 (vi)–B5, E5, and a measure of rest follow. The buildup of musical tension, intensified by the rhythmic wah-wah licks of Gtr. 2, makes for a dramatic effect in measure 6 when Gtr. 4 enters with thundering power chords that continue through measure 10. Paisley (Gtr. 1) transitions to the open position of the E major pentatonic scale in measures 6–9 while employing his usual intelligent note selection to nail the root of every chord. As Gtrs. 1 & 4 smack sustained E5 chords in measure 10, Gtr. 2 wraps up the intro with the funky octave E note pattern, ending on the open sixth (E) string on beat 1 of measure 11. Complementing the move, Gtr. 1 glisses from B5 on beat 4 of measure 10 to E5 on beat 1 of measure 11.

Performance Tip: Execute the double-string bend of C#/A by Gtr. 3 in measure 3 with the middle and ring fingers, low to high.

Fig. 33

*City noises fade out as music fades in over next 5 meas.

**Chord symbols reflect basic harmony.

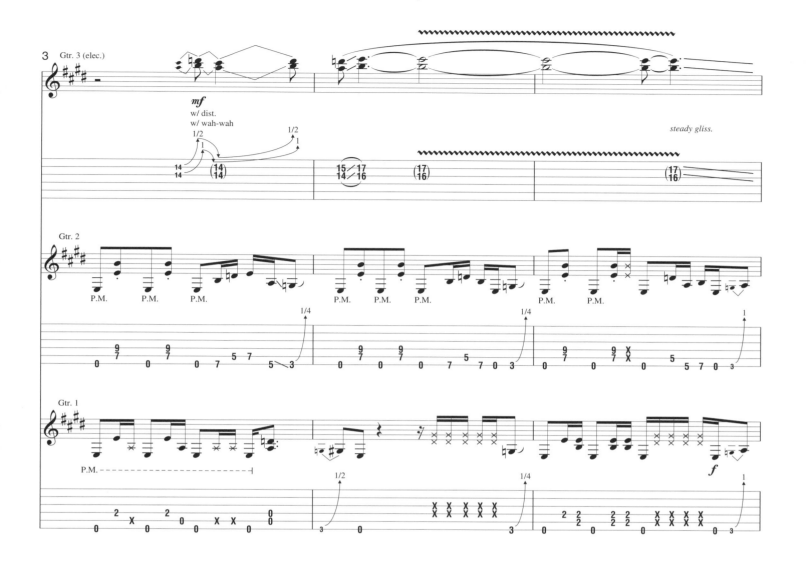

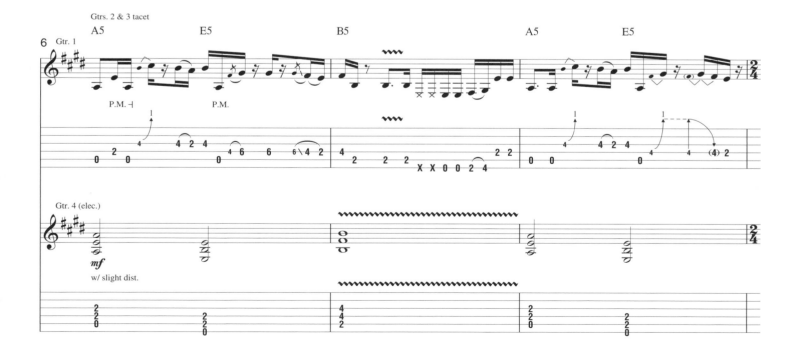

Figure 34—Verse 1

The 15-measure verse contains a favorite Paisley harmonic device of the vi (C#m) chord along with standard I (E), IV (A), and V (B) changes: E5, E5, A5, A5, E5, E5, B5, B5, C#m, C#m, A, A, E, B5, and E. Check out how it adds uplift after the B5 as well as producing a degree of musical tension that is released on the A5 chord that in turn moves the progression forward to the E5 chord in measure 13 for eventual I–V–I resolution.

Gtr. 2 (Paisley?) continues to drive the rhythm section straight ahead with a similar syncopated pattern of 5ths with the root note (mostly) on string 5, similar to the intro. Gtr. 3 accompanies with 5ths containing the root note on string 6, combining with Gtr. 2 for a thick, bassy growl. Observe how Gtr. 6 enters in measure 9 of the C#m chord with long, sustained 5ths through measure 15 that form a kind of musical "glue," holding the syncopated parts together and highlighting the change to the dramatic minor chord.

Performance Tip: Use steady down- and upstrokes for Gtrs. 2 and 3.

Fig. 34

Verse

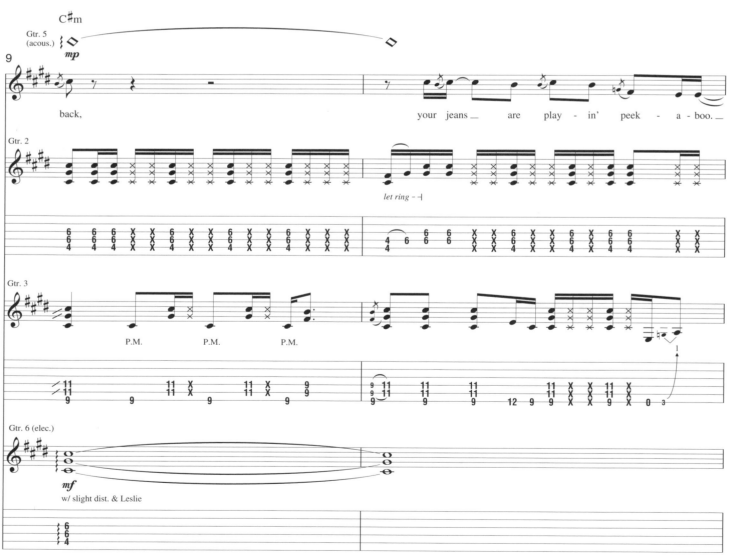

Figure 35—Guitar Solo

As befits his enormous talent, Paisley (Gtr. 1) is able to cram a lot of musical info into a short span of time. Within four measures of A5 (IV)–E5 (I), B5 (V), A5–E5, and B5–C#m (vi)–B5, he slithers through the E Ionian mode, with the inclusion of the G (♭3rd) note for some "tang," featuring dynamics of register and phrasing. In addition, he naturally pays close attention to the chord changes, picking every root at the very least. As is also his "calling card," he starts in the lower frequencies in measure 1 and leaps to the upper reaches of the scale in measure 2. He then repeats the process in measures 3 and 4, even going higher to fret 12 to build extra intensity, before zipping down the scale in the open position on beats 3 and 4 of measure 4.

Notice how every chord change receives individual and special attention. For example, after bending the G (♭7th) to A (root) on string 6 followed by the fretted A on string 3 at fret 2 in measure 1 over the A change, Paisley trills the G# (3rd) and E (root) notes over the E chord, punctuated with the open second (B) and first (E) strings struck as a double stop that chimes like a resonating bell. In measure 2, he picks the root-octave B, D# (3rd), and F# (5th) notes and then executes a snaky bend from C# (2nd) to D (♭3rd), released to C# and ending up on B. In measure 4, he plays identical, quicksilver pull-offs on strings 1–4 in open position of the E major scale that neatly imply the C#m and B5 chords.

Gtr. 2, taking a much more secondary and subordinate role, nonetheless contributes a significant flowing counterpoint line from the E major scale in the lower register, dotted with carefully placed 5ths to mark the passing harmony. The combination with Gtr. 1 results in a gracefully propulsive succession of melodic and harmonic ideas.

Performance Tip: Play the pull-offs in measure 4 with the ring and index fingers.

66 Full Band

67 Slow Demo
Gtr. 1   meas. 1–4

Fig. 35

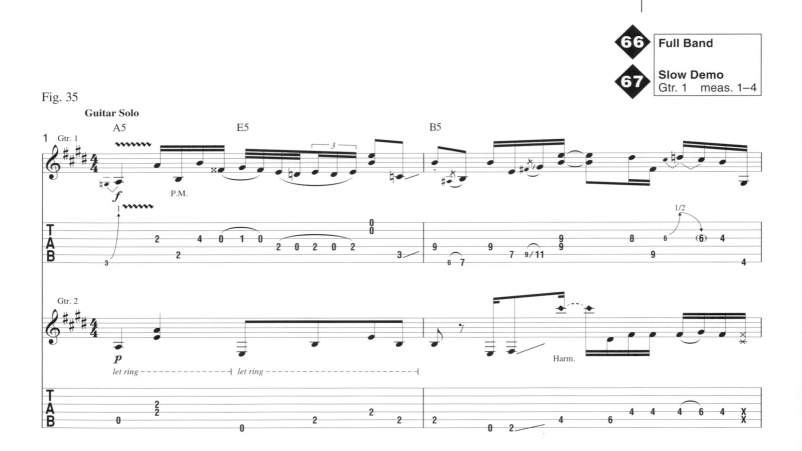

Figure 36—Outro

Paisley arranges measures 1–8 similarly to the verse with E5 (I), E5, A (IV)–E, B5 (V), A–E, C#m (vi)–B5, A, and A chords that function to create a sense of continuity with the chorus (not shown). In measures 1 and 2, Gtr. 2 plays a funky chordal pattern similar to the intro and verse in order to maintain groove and promote forward motion. In measures 3–8, Gtr. 2 plays sustained 5ths, relative to each chord change, as dynamic contrast in anticipation for the busy syncopating E5 tonality in measures 9–22 that contain various funky vamps to the fade out.

Gtr. 1 (Paisley) starts off in measures 3 and 4 with a reprise of the melody heard more extensively in the intro. Not coincidentally, the chord changes are almost identical to the intro, but notice that the solo begins on the A (IV) chord, a harmonic decision that automatically adds to the momentum. As opposed to the intro, however, here Paisley shows his advanced skills at negotiating the chord changes with the appropriate scale or chord-tone choices in measures 5–8. Over the A chord in measure 5, he plays a quick and hip A Mixolydian pattern followed with the E composite blues scale (Mixolydian mode plus blues scale) over the E change for a pungent whiff of the blues. Descending open-string pull-offs in measure 6 (in unusual 2/4 time) brilliantly implies the C#m and B5 changes, while the one-step bend from G (♭7th) to A (root) in conjunction with the C# (3rd) in measure 7 of the A chord makes short work of nailing the harmony. In measure 8 over the same change, he skips around the A composite blues scale with a funky feel setting up the resolution to the low E (root) string in measure 9 over the E5 chord where he dramatically and dynamically rests for two measures.

Paisley sounds as if he is just enjoying himself too much as the outro vamps and struts to the fade. Romping from one end of the fingerboard to the other with a mash-up of E scales and chord tones, he makes his Tele growl and snarl in counterpoint to the funky rhythm of Gtr. 2. His approach is actually quite simple, however: he creates musical tension through the repetition of riffs and motifs and then releases it with a flurry of notes. An example of the former is found in measures 11 and 12 where he rakes the open first (root) and second (5th) strings in conjunction with the A (4th) note on string 3 and follows with rumbling bass notes and a slinky, behind-the-nut bend in the open position of the E minor pentatonic scale in measures 12–14. An example of his note flurries occurs in measures 15–17 as Paisley tightens the musical screws with dyads in 4ths that briefly imply E, E7, A, D, and G changes in syncopated phrasing before breaking out with hot licks from the E composite blues scale in a variety of positions. At the same time, he makes sure to hit the E (root) note with regularity. Additionally, observe in measures 13–14 and 19–22 how Gtr. 3 sneaks in with a rippling trill to the E (root) note at fret 7 on string 5 in the former and a long bend from A (4th) to B (5th) in conjunction with the E at fret 17 on string 2 and vibratoed like crazy in the latter. Hoo-ee!

Performance Tip: To execute the behind-the-nut pre-bend in measure 14, push the D string down behind the nut a full step before you pick it, and then release it after the attack.

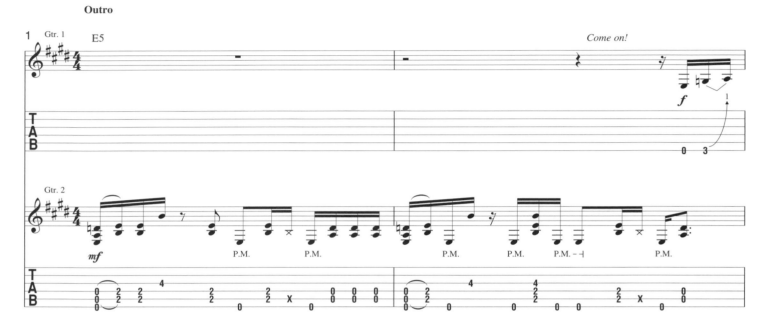

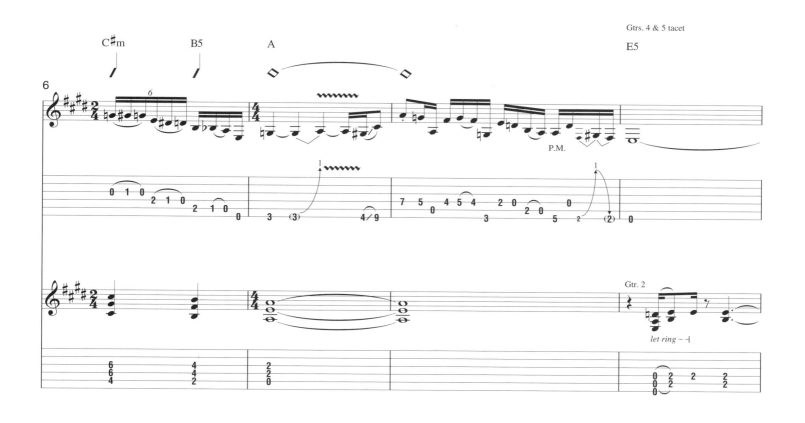

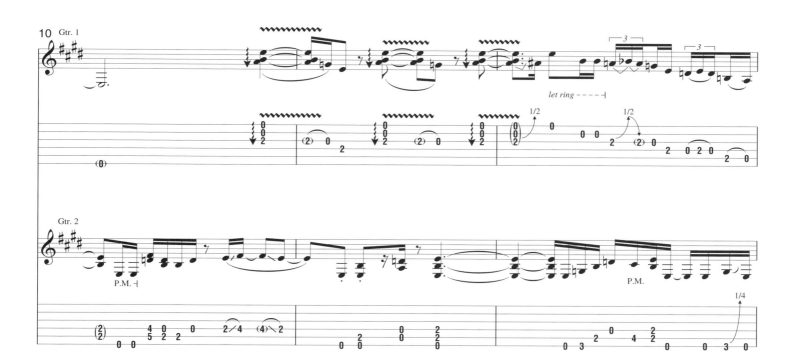

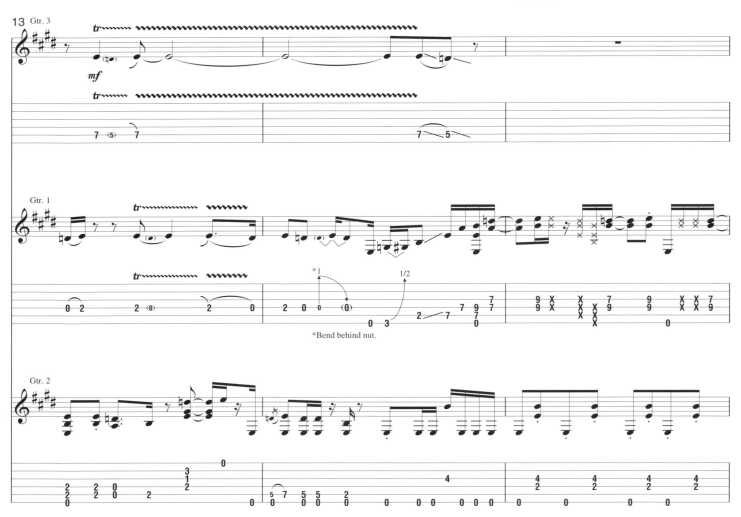

*Bend behind nut.

TIME WARP

(*Time Well Wasted*, 2005)
Words and Music by Brad Paisley and Frank Rogers

As the legitimate musical heir to the pioneering hot country guitarist Jimmy Bryant, Paisley takes every opportunity he can to "air out" his chops on an instrumental barn-burner. "Time Warp," with steel guitarist Michael "Mike Dee" Johnson, can take its right-ful place among the cleanest, fastest, and most thrilling numbers cut by Bryant and his partner, steeler Speedy West, as well as Joe Maphis and the modern "Nashville Cats" who followed.

Figure 37—Section A

Paisley (Gtr. 1) does a better than passable job of following in the footsteps of one of his heroes, the late, legendary country-jazz guitarist Hank Garland, in the nine measures of section A. After a pickup measure, he navigates with grace and consummate technical ability the jazzy chord changes of Amaj7 (I), D#°7 (#iv°), Bm9 (ii), and E7♭9 (V) that repeat two times. Utilizing the A major scale (Ionian mode) with one deviation, he invents light, breezy melodies while acknowledging each change with logical note selection. In measures 2 and 6 over the Amaj7 chord, he emphasizes the major tonality-defining C# (3rd), among lesser scale tones, while in measures 3 and 7 over the D#°7 (D#–F#–A–C) chord, he sustains the F# (♭3rd) that distinguishes the change. For the Bm9 in measure 4, Paisley nips the A (♭7th) and B (root) notes, but in measure 8, he opts to create soft musical tension by avoiding the root, ♭3rd (D), and ♭7th. The result makes for greater impact in measure 9 of E7 where he resolves conclusively with an E7 triple stop (D/G#/E).

Performance Tip: Use the middle, ring, and index fingers to access the G♭, B♭, and D notes for the downstroke in measures 5 and 6.

Fig. 37

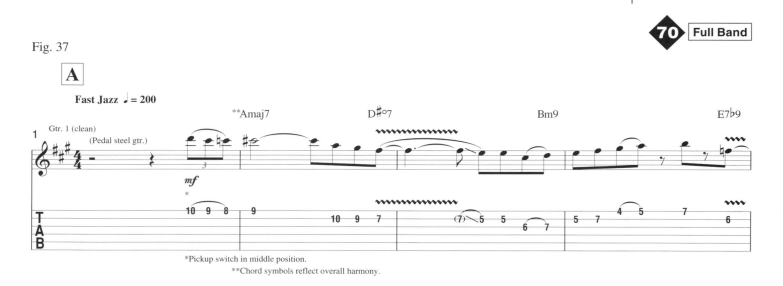

*Pickup switch in middle position.
**Chord symbols reflect overall harmony.

***Pickup switch in bridge position.

Figure 38—Section B

The blinding speed with which Paisley (Gtr. 1) blasts through the changes in the 16 measures of section B is downright frightening. Contributing to the stunning, headlong rush to the "finish line" following the lilting jazz of section A is the chord progression. The changes in measures 1–4 of A5 (I), C5 (♭III), D5 (IV), and A repeat twice and appear again in measures 9–12, containing great momentum and power. In between in measures 5–8 are F5 (♭VI), F5, E5 (V), and E5 chords that function as a dynamic buffer.

Check out how Paisley creates a "head" utilizing the A, C, D, and A Mixolydian modes in measures 1–4 and 9–12 in related patterns that each contain the open fifth (A), fourth (D), and third (G) strings as a unifying element. In measures 5–6, he uses the F major chord tones of F (root), A (3rd), and C (5th) in sequence that automatically provide a rudimentary melody, forward motion, and a harmonic outline. In addition, notice how Paisley bends the C to D (6th) on beat 2 of measure 6 to extend the harmony. More importantly, he bends the G (2nd) to A on beat 4 as it strongly leads to resolution on the E5 change in measure 7. In measure 8, he ends with half-step bends from C♯ (6th) to D (♭7th) that encourages movement to the A change in measure 9. In a similar manner, ending measure 12 on C (♭3rd) of beat 4 creates a degree of musical tension that advances motion to section C (not shown).

Performance Tip: Use the index and ring fingers for the hammer-ons and pull-offs in measures 1–4 and 9–12.

Fig. 38

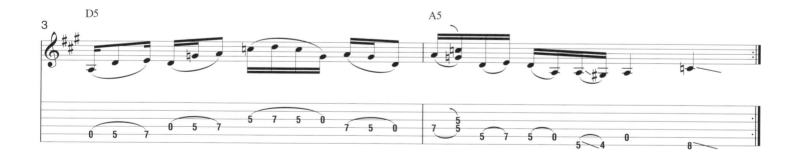

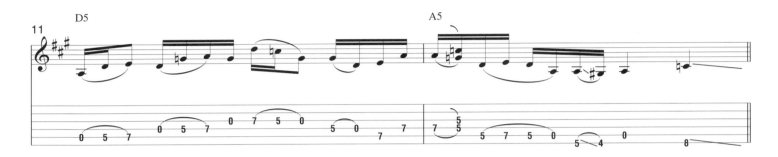

Figure 39—Section E

Realizing that non-stop speeding on the strings can become tedious despite the skill and musical expression involved, Paisley trots out welcome interruptions along the way. The nine measures of section E contain dynamic stop time every two measures up to measure 7 of G5 (♭VII) in 2/4 time. Observe that the new chords add obvious contrast to the tune along with the change of rhythm. In measures 1 and 5, they consist of F5 (♭VI)–G5, and in measure 3, they are F5–E5 (V). Measures 8–9 resolve to the E chord that drives steadily forward without the stop time. In measures 1–2, Paisley (Gtr. 1) utilizes the G composite blues scale (Mixolydian mode plus blues scale) to form his "response" to the "call" of the chords, hitting root notes as he does throughout the changes. In measures 3–4, he switches to the E composite blues scale and inserts a nasty-sounding triple stop of of G/D/B♭ (♭3rd/♭7th/♭5th) for musical tension resolved in the stop time chords of measure 5. Continuing through the G change in measures 6 and 7, Paisley plays a long, fast, arcing, "bluegrass-type" run from the G composite blues scale that functions as a climax of section E while leading smoothly down the fingerboard in the open position to the E (root) note in measure 8 of the E chord. Not content to let the progression "peter out" in the usual manner, he feels compelled to add back in a little tension with an F#/C# (2nd/6th) dyad sustained across the bar line of measures 8 and 9 before "glissing out" with the E note at fret 7 on string 5 in conjunction with the open 6th string.

Performance Tip: Play the triple stop in measure 4 with the middle, index, and ring fingers, low to high.

Fig. 39

Full Band

Slow Demo
Gtr. 1   meas. 1–2,
5–7

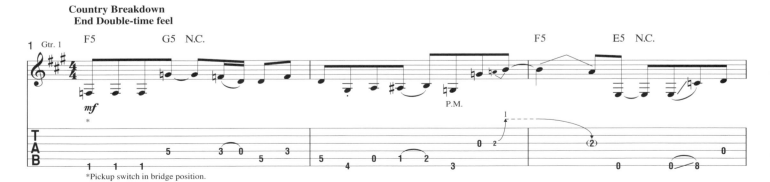

*Pickup switch in bridge position.

Figure 40—Section J (Guitar Solo)

With a radical change in tempo from 200 to 67 beats per minute and the time signature from 4/4 to 6/8, the play-on-words of the title "Time Warp" becomes even clearer with section J. The 16-measure progression is a virtual duplication of section B, though the much slower "slow blues" tempo makes it feel more dramatic, a fact that Paisley (Gtr. 2) exploits for one of his most heartfelt solos. Getting right into the spirit of the occasion, he relies almost exclusively on the A minor pentatonic scale in the root and root-octave positions for a grittier and bluesier sound than what usually flows from his strings. That said, he can hardly resist acknowledging the chord changes as in measure 2 over the C5 (♭III) chord, where he sustains and vibratos the C (root) note. In measure 3 over the D5 (IV) chord, he bends the C (♭7th) to D (root) and the E (2nd) to F♯ (3rd) to imply a D major tonality. Sometimes he even goes outside of his scale of choice to accomplish the harmonic navigation, as in measures 7 and 8, where he plays D9 and A9 chord voicings to intensify the D and A (I) changes, respectively.

Starting in measure 9 and continuing through the end of the section, Paisley trades in his white cowboy hat for a pair of dark "shades" and plays his most biting and lyrical blues licks. Most impressive are his bends in measures 9 and 10 over the F7 (♭VI) chord that prominently nail the sweet A (3rd) via the G (9th) on strings 1 and 2 as he plays noticeably behind the beat. Other points of interest are found in measure 11 over the E7 (V) chord, where he utilizes an E major triad in conjunction with notes from the E composite blues scale. Observe the hip, tension-inducing bend from the G♯ (3rd) to A (4th) across the bar line of measure 12 that is released back to G♯ leading to resolution on the E (root) note on beat 2. In addition, check out the cool harmony bend in measure 14 over the C5 chord that produces G/E (5th/3rd) followed by Paisley releasing the bend on string 2 in microtonal increments that creates stunning tension through dissonance. A blur of licks in the root position of the A blues scale in measure 15 over the D5 chord provides dynamic contrast while goosing the progression forward to completion in measure 16 over the A chord. There, a tumbling run down the root position of the A minor pentatonic scale does not resolve but instead carries the burst of energy directly forward to section K (not shown).

Performance Tip: Paisley likely executes the bend on string 2 in measure 3 with a B-bender in conjunction with bending string 3 by hand. In place of that, try bending string 3 with the middle finger followed immediately by string 2 bent with the ring finger. It will not be easy…

Fig. 40

J

Guitar Solo
Slow Blues ♩ = 67

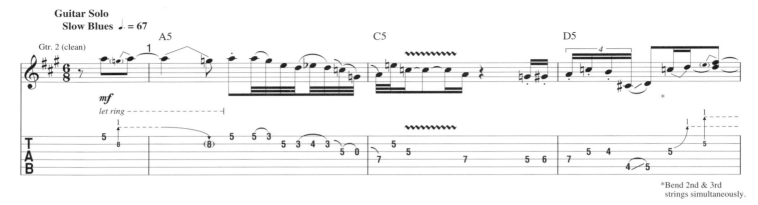

*Bend 2nd & 3rd
strings simultaneously.

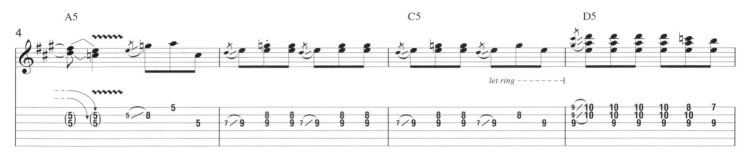

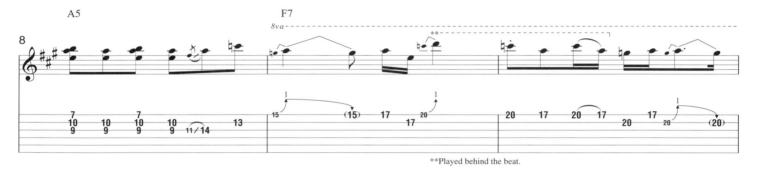

**Played behind the beat.

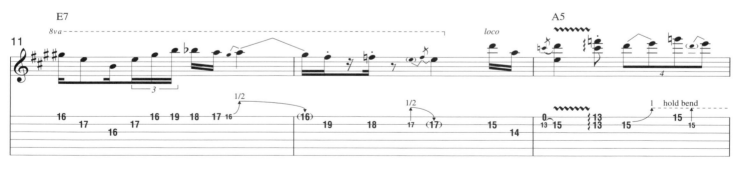

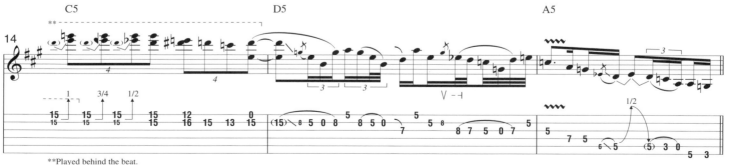

**Played behind the beat.

THE WORLD
(*Time Well Wasted*, 2005)
Words and Music by Brad Paisley, Kelley Lovelace and Lee Thomas Miller

Besides hitting #1 on the country charts, #81 on the Pop 100, and #45 on the *Billboard* Top 100 charts, the lead-off track on Paisley's breakout album gave him bona fide street credit to rock "The World."

Figure 41—Verse

The rockabilly-inspired 16-measure verse is comprised of two identical eight-measure progressions containing pairs of E (I), B (V), C#m (vi), and A (IV) chords. The addition of the vi adds an element of melancholy that Paisley subtly exploits with his vocal delivery. As Gtr. 2, he plays rudimentary voicings and related scale tones that would even suffice to carry the rhythm in a trio. In measures 1–2 and 9–10 of the E change, he builds his harmony around the basic E/B dyad at fret 2 and the C# (6th) note on string 5 at fret 4. Notice how he also utilizes the C# note in conjunction with the A changes in measures 7 and 8, where it functions as the major tonality-defining 3rd. In measures 15 and 16, however, he includes the C (♭3rd) and B (2nd), respectively, to create a little bass run up to the C# for momentum.

To help keep the rhythm boogying as established in the intro (not shown), Gtr. 1 plays big, open-position E chords with alternating 6ths (C#) on string 5 in measures 1 and 2. The remainder of the chord changes are given a propulsive boost by having each measure begin with the root note played twice on beat 1 and one time on beat 3 followed by the strummed voicing.

Performance Tip: For measures 1 and 2 as played by Gtr. 1, form the E major chord, low to high, with the middle, ring, and index fingers. Access the alternating C# with the pinky.

Fig. 41

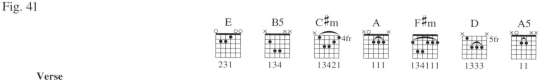

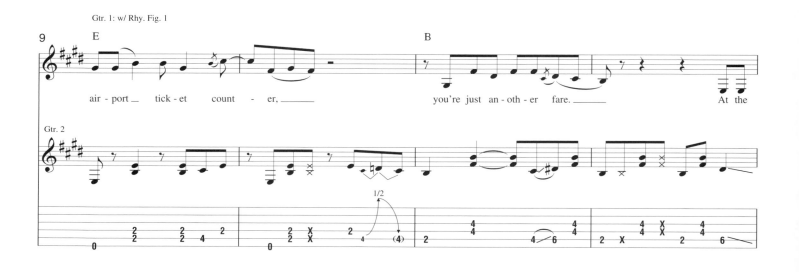

Figure 42—Chorus

The 12-measure chorus bears a harmonic and rhythmic resemblance to the verse and helps to maintain the driving energy of the song. It consists of pairs of E (I), B5 (V), C#m (vi), A (IV), F#m (ii), and B5 chords fleshed out with three guitar parts. Paisley (Gtr. 2) mainly plays "power chords" with an added octave note on top. Observe how he fills between his vocals in measures 1 and 2 (following his exhortation "…is to the world" in the preceding pre-chorus, not shown) along with measures 5–8. For the first one, he combines the E (root) and B (5th) notes with a gliss from F# (2nd) to G# (3rd) with the E/B dyad in a syncopated, horn-like manner that operates as a counterpoint to the chugging rhythm.

For the longer, second fill, he employs a number of musical techniques to create a compressed instrumental "break" that rises and falls in pitch with a moving bass line and stages the action for the punch line, "…baby, you are the world," in measures 11 and 12. Check out his use of C# (root) on string 5, preceding C#/G# (root/5th) in measure 5, followed by an arpeggiated C#5 chord in measure 6 in conjunction with the C# glissed to B (root of B5 inserted on beat 4) and resolving to the open fifth (A) string and A/E (root/5th) in measure 7. The bluesy bass line of C (b3rd) to C# (3rd) preceding A/E on beats 3 and 4 of measure 7 adds a dynamic "bump in the road" before Paisley resolves the A change with the open fifth string and the A/E dyad.

Performance Tip: In measure 1, slide from F# to G# on string 5 with the ring finger and then fret the A/E dyad with the index finger.

Fig. 42

Figure 43—Guitar Solo

The progression in the 16-measure guitar solo is virtually the same as the verse except for one significant chord change. Instead of being comprised of two eight-measure sections, measure 14 contains a D (♭VII), as opposed to a second measure of C#m (vi). The result contributes mightily to a whoosh of momentum on the way to the climactic measures. The D is an uplifting half step above C#m, leading to the A chords in measures 15–16 that could be seen as a muscular I (D)–V (A) move.

Paisley, as is often his wont, fits a lot of musical info into 16 measures, mostly through the technique of "playing the changes." In measures 1–2 over the E chord, he repeatedly picks the open sixth (E) string, almost as a pedal tone, in conjunction with the fretted E on string 5 at fret 7 to produce a big, fat E tonality. After banging on string 6 with the F♯ (2nd) to G♯ (3rd) notes, he slides up to B (root) on beat 1 of measure 3 and then makes a huge, dynamic leap with the D♯/B (3rd/root) and C♯/A (9th/♭7th) dyads at frets 16 and 14, respectively, that imply B major and B9 voicings. In measure 4, however, he opts to insert a jolt of musical tension with E/B (4th/root) bent one step to F♯/C♯ (5th/9th) with searing vibrato. He shifts to the root position of the C♯ blues scale in measures 5–6 over the C♯m chord and emphasizes the minor tonality while keeping the pot boiling with rippling triplets. Ending on E, the ♭3rd of C♯m but the 5th of A, on beat 4 of measure 6 makes for a logical transition to measures 7–8. Following with a dynamic drop of register down to the open position of the A Mixolydian mode, Paisley maintains a "string" of pumping single-note lines while likewise defining the harmony.

The whole point of measures 9–16 is for him to build a relentless head of stream to the end. His strategy is simple but thrillingly effective. He begins on the open sixth string of the E Mixolydian mode, twangs and emphasizes the bluesy D (♭7th) on the open fourth string, and climbs the fingerboard, finishing high above, rocking and rolling in the root-octave position of the E Mixolydian mode. On the way up, he has a brief stop over the B (V) change in measures 11–12 where he combines single-note lines from the B composite blues scale and dyads relative to B major. To his credit, he works the key change with the skill of a magician so that the flow of his solo is uninterrupted. In a similar vein, in measure 13 over the C♯m chord, he dips into the E minor pentatonic scale for an edge of dissonance. It is highlighted by a brief, blazing, raspy upstroke on B/G/E (major 7th/♭5th/♭3rd) that could be seen as an E minor triad, while advancing the solo to measure 14 and the E Mixolydian mode over the D change. Observe the classic blues double-string, quarter-step bend of G/C♯ (4th/major 7th) that functions as a slight pause in the action along with a shot of musical tension before Paisley cracks it all open in measures 15–16. Whipping back and forth between dyads in 3rds of C♯/A and B/G that imply A and A9, respectively, he sounds like a modern-day Chuck Berry "ringing a bell," by way of Nashville.

Performance Tip: In measures 15–16, use the ring finger for the C♯/A dyad and the index finger for the B/G dyad.

79	Full Band
80	Slow Demo
	Gtr. 5 meas. 5–8

Fig. 43

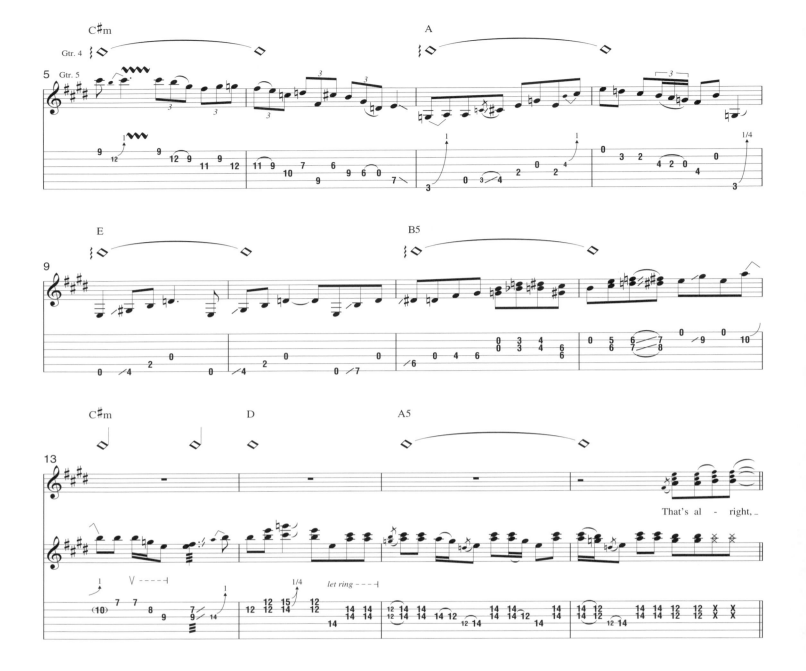

Figure 44—Outro

With the rhythm Gtrs. 3, 4 & 6 vamping out on E (I) for 28 measures, Paisley (Gtr. 5) indulges his whimsy while also propelling the song toward an appropriate and satisfying conclusion. Be sure to see that, following Paisley playing Rhy. Fig. 1 in measures 1–8 that confirms the E major tonality in conjunction with the open E major chord sustained by Gtr. 6 in measures 5–8, the progression takes a turn to the harmonically ambiguous. Consequently, Paisley takes advantage of the situation to eventually step outside the E major scale that serves his purpose well in measures 7–18. Especially effective in producing musical tension necessary over a I-chord vamp, however, are a number of long, arcing bends. The one-step variety from the A (4th) note in the open position on string 3 at fret 2 in measures 9–10 that hits B (5th) and B♭ (♭5th) is likely executed with a G-bender and resolves handsomely to the G♯ (major 3rd) and E (root) in measure 11. Similarly, the half-step bend from C♯ (6th) to D (♭7th) on string 1 at fret 9 in measure 14 creates and opens the door for tension in measures 15–16 that Paisley resolves in measure 17 with the open sixth (E) string. In a surprising move, he quickly follows with a fun, howling "dive bomb" of the E lowered one-half step to E♭ (major 7th) by pushing forward on the neck (Again: *Not particularly recommended on any guitar other than a solid Tele*) before glissing up the neck to fret 12.

Arriving at his new location on the fingerboard, Paisley scampers up and down the root-octave position of the E Dorian mode in measures 19–20. Though theoretically a minor mode, the effect here is more bluesy than minor, and the dynamic contrast to what preceded is also a great prelude to the chords and syncopated double stops that follow. Beginning with what is essentially an Em7 voicing in measure 21, Paisley continues on with honking dyads and triple stops in the root-octave position of the E Dorian mode. Observe the musical tension of G/D (♭3rd/♭7th) combined with G/C♯/G (3rd/6th/♭3rd) in measure 23 followed by the hip sequence in measure 24 of G/C♯ (♭3rd/6th), F♯/B/G (9th/5th/♭3rd), E/B/G (root/5th/♭3rd), C♯/A/E (6th/4th/root), and B/G (bent a bluesy half and quarter steps, respectively) that continues in a similar fashion through measures 25–26. Mercifully, the increasing tension is resolved in measures 27–28 with the implied voicings of G♯m (iii), F♯m (ii), and E (I).

Performance Tip: Anchor the index finger at fret 12 in order to access the various forms with the ring and pinky fingers of measures 21–26.

81 **Full Band**

82 **Slow Demo**
Gtr. 5   meas. 19–20

Fig. 44

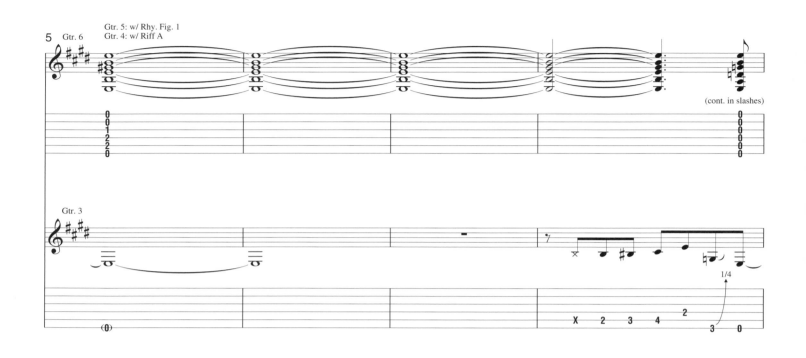

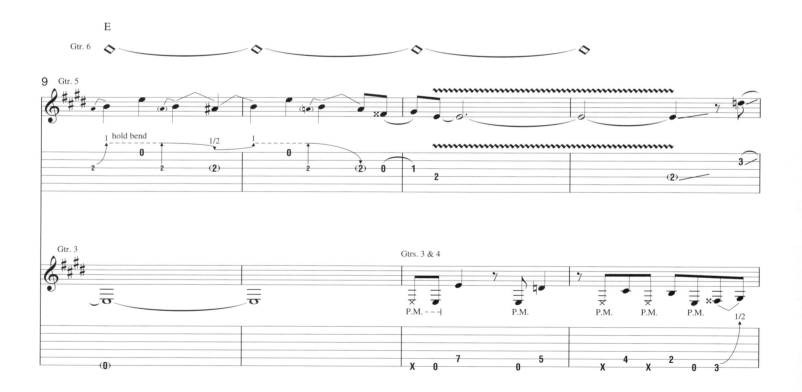

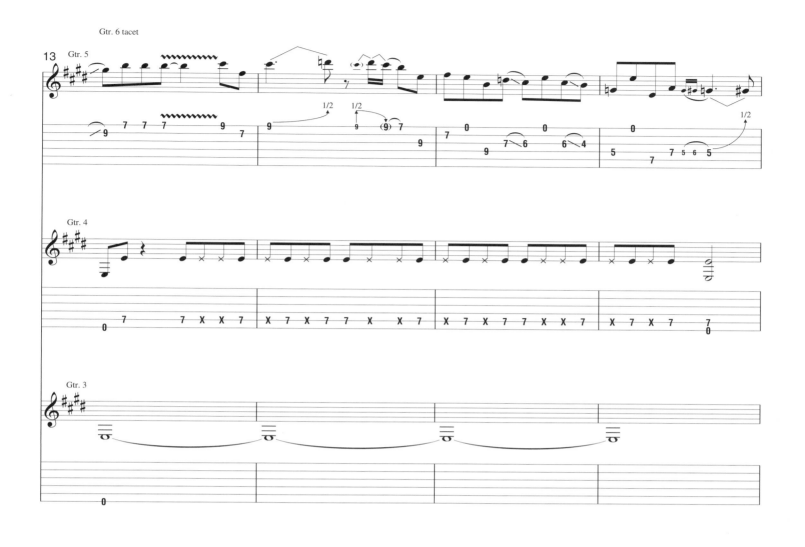

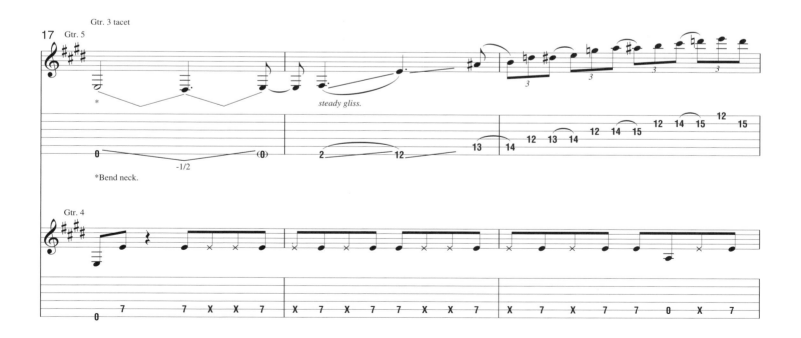

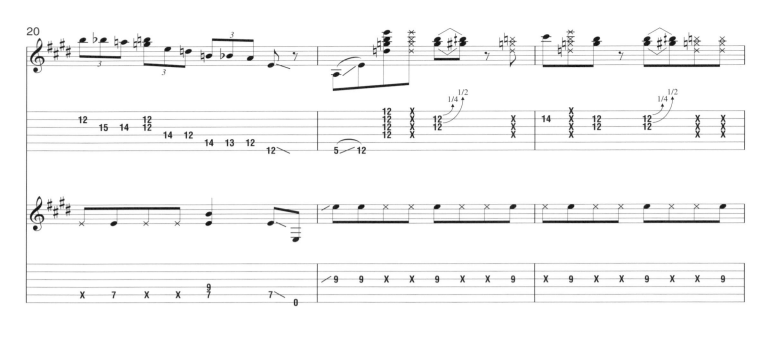

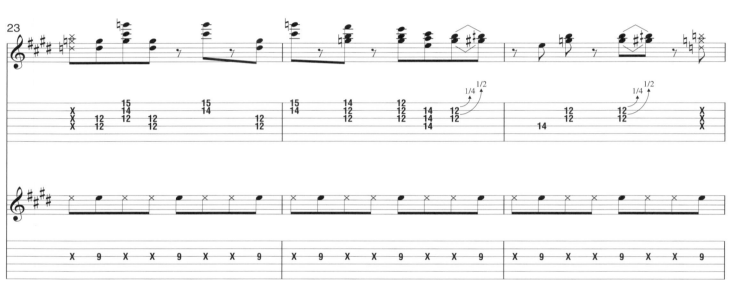

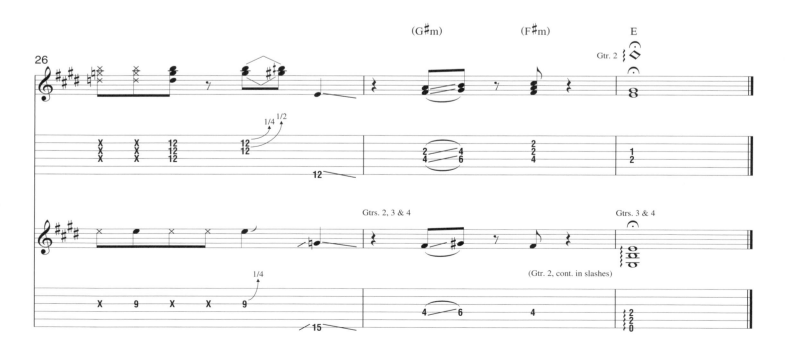

GUITAR NOTATION LEGEND

Guitar music can be notated three different ways: on a *musical staff*, in *tablature*, and in *rhythm slashes*.

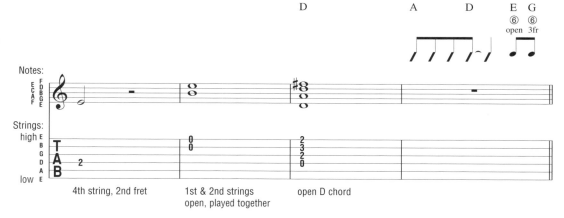

RHYTHM SLASHES are written above the staff. Strum chords in the rhythm indicated. Use the chord diagrams found at the top of the first page of the transcription for the appropriate chord voicings. Round noteheads indicate single notes.

THE MUSICAL STAFF shows pitches and rhythms and is divided by bar lines into measures. Pitches are named after the first seven letters of the alphabet.

TABLATURE graphically represents the guitar fingerboard. Each horizontal line represents a string, and each number represents a fret.

4th string, 2nd fret

1st & 2nd strings open, played together

open D chord

Definitions for Special Guitar Notation

HALF-STEP BEND: Strike the note and bend up 1/2 step.

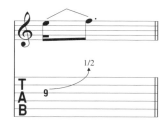

WHOLE-STEP BEND: Strike the note and bend up one step.

GRACE NOTE BEND: Strike the note and immediately bend up as indicated.

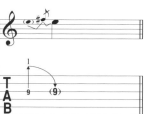

SLIGHT (MICROTONE) BEND: Strike the note and bend up 1/4 step.

BEND AND RELEASE: Strike the note and bend up as indicated, then release back to the original note. Only the first note is struck.

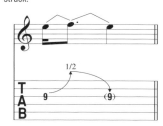

PRE-BEND: Bend the note as indicated, then strike it.

PRE-BEND AND RELEASE: Bend the note as indicated. Strike it and release the bend back to the original note.

UNISON BEND: Strike the two notes simultaneously and bend the lower note up to the pitch of the higher.

VIBRATO: The string is vibrated by rapidly bending and releasing the note with the fretting hand.

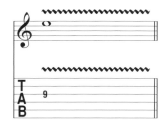

WIDE VIBRATO: The pitch is varied to a greater degree by vibrating with the fretting hand.

HAMMER-ON: Strike the first (lower) note with one finger, then sound the higher note (on the same string) with another finger by fretting it without picking.

PULL-OFF: Place both fingers on the notes to be sounded. Strike the first note and without picking, pull the finger off to sound the second (lower) note.

LEGATO SLIDE: Strike the first note and then slide the same fret-hand finger up or down to the second note. The second note is not struck.

SHIFT SLIDE: Same as legato slide, except the second note is struck.

TRILL: Very rapidly alternate between the notes indicated by continuously hammering on and pulling off.

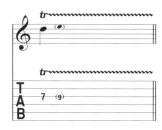

TAPPING: Hammer ("tap") the fret indicated with the pick-hand index or middle finger and pull off to the note fretted by the fret hand.

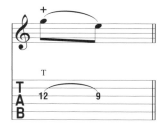

NATURAL HARMONIC: Strike the note while the fret-hand lightly touches the string directly over the fret indicated.

PINCH HARMONIC: The note is fretted normally and a harmonic is produced by adding the edge of the thumb or the tip of the index finger of the pick hand to the normal pick attack.

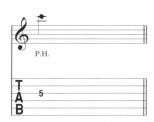

HARP HARMONIC: The note is fretted normally and a harmonic is produced by gently resting the pick hand's index finger directly above the indicated fret (in parentheses) while the pick hand's thumb or pick assists by plucking the appropriate string.

PICK SCRAPE: The edge of the pick is rubbed down (or up) the string, producing a scratchy sound.

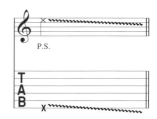

MUFFLED STRINGS: A percussive sound is produced by laying the fret hand across the string(s) without depressing, and striking them with the pick hand.

PALM MUTING: The note is partially muted by the pick hand lightly touching the string(s) just before the bridge.

RAKE: Drag the pick across the strings indicated with a single motion.

TREMOLO PICKING: The note is picked as rapidly and continuously as possible.

ARPEGGIATE: Play the notes of the chord indicated by quickly rolling them from bottom to top.

VIBRATO BAR DIVE AND RETURN: The pitch of the note or chord is dropped a specified number of steps (in rhythm), then returned to the original pitch.

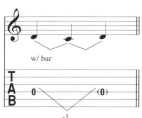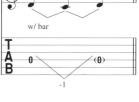

VIBRATO BAR SCOOP: Depress the bar just before striking the note, then quickly release the bar.

VIBRATO BAR DIP: Strike the note and then immediately drop a specified number of steps, then release back to the original pitch.

Additional Musical Definitions

 (accent) • Accentuate note (play it louder).

(accent) • Accentuate note with great intensity.

(staccato) • Play the note short.

⊓ • Downstroke

V • Upstroke

D.S. al Coda • Go back to the sign (𝄋), then play until the measure marked "*To Coda*," then skip to the section labelled "**Coda**."

D.C. al Fine • Go back to the beginning of the song and play until the measure marked "*Fine*" (end).

Rhy. Fig. • Label used to recall a recurring accompaniment pattern (usually chordal).

Riff • Label used to recall composed, melodic lines (usually single notes) which recur.

Fill • Label used to identify a brief melodic figure which is to be inserted into the arrangement.

Rhy. Fill • A chordal version of a Fill.

tacet • Instrument is silent (drops out).

 • Repeat measures between signs.

 • When a repeated section has different endings, play the first ending only the first time and the second ending only the second time.

NOTE: Tablature numbers in parentheses mean:
1. The note is being sustained over a system (note in standard notation is tied), or
2. The note is sustained, but a new articulation (such as a hammer-on, pull-off, slide or vibrato) begins, or
3. The note is a barely audible "ghost" note (note in standard notation is also in parentheses).